A Sunset Book

How to Plan and Build

YOUR
FIREPLACE

THE COVER

Top, left: Bold fireplace with concrete blocks and steel hood. See also page 61 (William Corlett, design). *Top, right:* Factory-built sheet metal fireplace in a low-budget home (Wendell Lovett, design; Dick Dawson, photo). *Bottom, left:* Kitchen-dining room hearth backs up against the living room fireplace shown on page 6 (Francis Constable, design; Ernest Braun, photo). *Bottom, right:* Detail from the fireplace shown on page 33. The burlap-covered wall has turned to gold (Ernest Braun, photo).

George Kosmak, design; Ernest Braun, photo

Metal-hooded fireplace occupies a recessed area in
the main, open room of this house. The massive stone
wall to the left contrasts with the 16-foot glass doors.
From the generous built-in sofa that surrounds the
hearth, you get a view of sky through ancient trees

A Sunset Book

How to Plan and Build

YOUR

FIREPLACE

By the editorial staffs of Sunset Books & Sunset Magazine

LANE BOOKS • MENLO PARK, CALIFORNIA

A. Quincy Jones, design; C. Cleveland, photo

Sixteenth Printing December 1972

Contents

Home is where the hearth is

When prehistoric man went cave-hunting, probably one of the first things he looked for in a vacant cave was the fire place. He doubtless examined the firepit with a very critical eye, poked around in the charcoal, and appraised the streak of soot running up the wall.

For fire was the center of his cavern life. He feared it, worshiped it, and used it as a servant. The flames lighted the black recesses of his cave. The fire kept him alive through the winter; and it thawed him when he returned, chilled from pursuing an evening's meal. It cooked and preserved his game.

Like the cave dweller, we of today recognize the fireplace as the heart and center of the home. We, too, put it to very practical uses—and in odd ways that would baffle our primitive ancestors. We use our hearths for many things—to roast venison and barbecue lamb, to broil hamburger, toast marshmallows and pop corn; we find it handy for disposing of old love letters, canceled checks, mortgages, and broken furniture and toys. Sometimes we use it to dry clothes, dogs, mittens, and children.

These are highly useful accomplishments for which we duly respect the fireplace, but we attach greater value to its subtler virtues that directly affect our well being. The warmth of the hearth and the hypnotic play of flame and shadow soothe our restless minds. In storming weather, we take heart from the flames' crackling defiance of the wind and rain. The fireside provides companionship for the lonely, and it radiates fellowship for the friendly gathering. Perhaps most of all in this electronic day, we value the hearth for its stubborn refusal to yield to the push-button. We sense that the log burning freely in the grate is a direct hand-me-down from the simple fellow who lived in a cave.

These virtues that seem so obvious to us today have not always been so warmly appreciated. Indeed, acceptance of the hearth into the home has had its ups and downs over the years.

The houses of the first settlers along the Eastern seaboard probably saw the fireplace reach the busiest point in its development. Many of the settlers came from mild-tempered climates in England, and the hostile Yankee winters inspired them to build massive fireplaces and chimneys. The family's life was clustered closely around the great hearth for light, warmth, and food. There, in the direct heat of the open fire, the incombustible housewife toiled with an array of grills, spits, and cranes and amber-glowing pots, pans, and skillets.

Then came an invention that relieved the wilted cook of some of her more hazardous tasks. The cast-iron range, which appeared in the late 1700's, seemed clearly superior to the fireplace in cooking efficiency and ease of use, and it soon pushed the hearth right out of the kitchen. The fireplace then took over heating the other rooms of the house, until it was shortly challenged by another development—the cast iron air-tight stove. This invention was much more efficient than the fireplace as a heating device. It was relatively light in weight, could be installed in almost any room, and didn't require a 5,000-pound masonry chimney.

Presently, the stove in its turn was elbowed aside by yet another invention—the central furnace. Developed with the spread of the new fuels, coal and later oil, it appealed to our grandfathers as superior to half a dozen stoves, or a dozen fireplaces. Many people concluded that the fireplace was obsolete and a wasteful luxury. So, for many bleak years, thousands of homes were built without a hearth, or with only a bogus fireplace and plaster logs.

After a while, people began to discover that they couldn't warm up to a warm-air outlet or a clanking radiator, and they missed the amiable warmth of the hearth; so they began to sneak fireplaces back into the house plans, for "supplementary heating," they said. In the last few years, fireplaces have also been welcomed back to the kitchen to cheer up that active room and to take over some of the more savory forms of cooking, too subtle for the modern precision range.

Today, the fireplace is an accepted and expected feature of the structural detail for most new homes. By the bold and artful use of line and material, it is being blended into the over-all plan so it takes its rightful place in the center of things, and looks as though it belonged right there.

In this book you will find how people of today are working the hearth into their homes. If you are planning to build or to remodel, or to buy a house already equipped with a hearth, or if you just like fireplaces, perhaps you will find in these pages some ideas you can put to good use.

Francis A. Constable, design; Ernest Braun, photo

Left: Warmth and cheer of this used-brick fireplace permeate the home. Floor-to-rafter height makes it appear part of house structure, not an afterthought. Hearth shared with dining room ties rooms together. Brick tones blend with walls

Anatomy of a fireplace

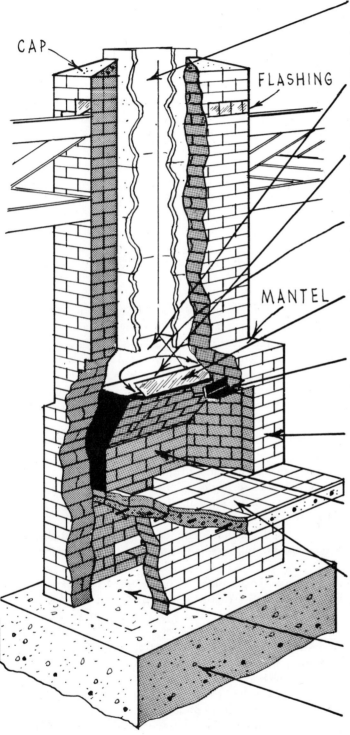

CAP

FLASHING

MANTEL

CHIMNEY FLUE

Smoke and combustion gases from the burning wood pass up the chimney inside a flue. Flues usually consist of large-diameter terra cotta pipe.

SMOKE CHAMBER

The smoke chamber acts as a funnel to compress the smoke and gases rising from the fire so they will squeeze into the chimney flue above.

SMOKE SHELF

A smoke shelf bounces stray downdrafts back up the chimney before they can neutralize the updraft and blow smoke into the room.

THROAT

The throat is a slot-like opening above the firebox, where flame, smoke, and combustion gases pass into the smoke chamber. It is usually fitted with a damper.

DAMPER

The damper is a steel or cast iron door that opens or closes the throat opening. Used to check and regulate draft, it prevents loss of heat up the chimney.

LINTEL

The lintel is a heavy steel brace that supports the masonry above the fireplace opening. Sometimes, it is incorporated in the damper assembly.

FACE

The masonry surrounding the fireplace opening is known as the fireplace "face." It may be built of various materials: brick, stone, concrete, tile, wood.

FIREBOX

The chamber where the fire is built is made of fire-resistant brick. Walls and back are slanted slightly to radiate heat out into the room.

HEARTH

Inner hearth of fire-resistant brick holds the burning fuel; outer hearth of tile, brick, etc., protects house flooring from heat, sparks. Supported by subhearth.

ASH PIT

Ashes are dumped through an opening in the hearth into the fireproof storage compartment below. Many fireplaces today are built without ash pits.

FOUNDATION

The fireplace and chimney structure has its own foundation. The concentrated weight of the masonry is usually carried by a reinforced concrete slab.

Planning your fireplace

When you sit down to plan your central fireplace, you may be surprised to find yourself working with a problem of some complexity.

If a fireplace were simply a living-room object that could be shoved against the wall like a radio, its planning would be as easy as putting on a log. But even the simplest metal fireplace becomes a permanent fixture once you knock a hole in your roof for the chimney—and a fireplace sets the tone for an entire room, perhaps a home. To make sure that your fireplace will create the atmosphere you have in mind, will look as though it belonged where it was built and was not pasted on or slipped in as an afterthought—you will want to study the problem from several angles.

DO YOU REALLY NEED ONE?

Honestly examine your reasons for wanting a fireplace and see if you would actually use it or if you might ignore it after its novelty had worn off. Since a fireplace often represents up to 5 per cent of the cost of your house, you had better convince yourself that you really need it.

The answer, of course, comes from your family's ways of living. How would the family use the fireplace? Does your family actually live in the living room or in some other room—say the kitchen? If you were forced to choose, would you select the living room over all the others?

How do you entertain? Formally or casually? Do you assemble guests in droves or two's and four's—to converse, play cards, or dance? Would a small or a spacious fireplace better suit your social requirements?

Will a single fireplace answer your needs? How about another one in a bedroom, the dining room, den, kitchen, or patio? How about using one chimney for two fireplaces back-to-back? Do you want the furnace features offered by a hot-air circulator? If you have a handyman's talents, perhaps you should consider installing a prefabricated fireplace and chimney. Or you might want to make rough-in provisions now for a fireplace to be built later.

HOW MUCH EMPHASIS?

Once you have soundly convinced yourself that you need a fireplace, your next problem is to decide how much emphasis you wish to give it.

Many people prefer a fireplace that is understressed, fitted modestly into a wall so it is an important feature of a room but not the dominant one. Some want a fireplace that is paired off with another center of attraction such as a bank of bookshelves or the view from a picture window. Others desire a fireplace that indisputably dominates the room, through its massive size, striking design, or unusual materials.

Design of the facing itself can be worked out either to accentuate or minimize the fireplace. If you want to blend your fireplace inconspicuously into the room, you can extend the mantel line to tie-in other elements such as shelving, counters, cabinets, or windows; or, you can extend the hearth to join with

Fireplace may be blended into elements of room design

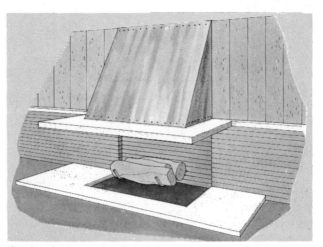

Or fireplace may be dramatized, room designed around it

steps, plant boxes, or built-in benches and couches. If you want to dramatize your fireplace, you can shape its lines to oppose those that mainly characterize the room. Thus, the angular form of a hood will emphasize the fireplace in a boxy room, strong vertical mortar joints will appear to raise a low ceiling, strong horizontal lines to widen a narrow room.

Materials may be selected to blend or contrast with those in the room's walls, floor, or cabinetwork. For an unobtrusive hearth, the facing may be covered over with the same stucco or paneling that blankets the walls; the soft tones of brick can be combined harmoniously with warm wood paneling. For a dominating fireplace, rough concrete, dressed stone, or shining metal can be used in contrast with bland veneers.

Emphasis may also be given by various structural devices. A cantilevered hearth dramatizes the facing. A fireplace built into a masonry wall or partition may seem to be a simple part of the wall; or the mass of the masonry itself may give the fireplace preeminence in the room. The hearth can also be tucked away in a corner, or angled across one with eye-catching results. For ultimate impact, nothing can approach the free-standing fireplace, alone in the middle of everything.

WHERE SHOULD YOU PUT IT?

Fireplaces are customarily located in the long wall of a room, but there is no iron-bound rule requiring this, and, if you want, you can center it in the short wall, or place it in a corner or even the middle of the floor.

Here are some of the factors that will influence your selection of a site.

Traffic Patterns: The flow of traffic through a room will definitely affect the choice of a location. You

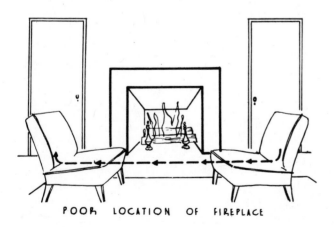

POOR LOCATION OF FIREPLACE

should avoid placing the fireplace where traffic from door to door passes through the room between furniture and fireplace. Also, it should be so placed that it will not force the firetender to trample over his guests when he brings in an armful of fuel from the wood pile.

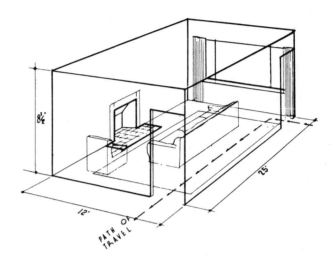

Furniture: Will the furniture you now have *and the pieces you plan to acquire* group easily around the fireplace? Will you and your guests be able to enjoy the fire without any neck stretching? Will the fire be just as enjoyable to two guests as to ten? Also, will there be room in front of the hearth to set a table for an intimate family supper?

Perhaps you own a dominating piece of furniture like a grand piano, a television set, or a decorator's piece. To keep it from quarreling with the fireplace for the center of attention, you may have to plan for orienting the room toward both it and the hearth or else pulling it into the hearth's circle. You may need the conciliatory services of a decorator to solve this contest.

Structural limitations: The location of a fireplace is often determined by conditions that restrict the location of the chimney. It is not unusual for a chimney to be limited to one or two possible sites because of factors that might affect its drawing capacity such as trees, nearby buildings, the roof line, or some topographic peculiarity on the landsite. Or, it may be necessary to use a single chimney to vent a furnace, kitchen range, barbecue, or additional fireplaces located in the basement, on the second floor, or outdoors. Perhaps you plan to add an outdoor fireplace later and you have only one or two possible sites for a patio.

Other complications to consider: placement of stairs around or in back of the chimney, fitting of a fireplace into a window wall, suitability of soil conditions for carrying the concentrated load of fire-place and chimney.

HOW BIG SHOULD IT BE?

The size of a fireplace opening is determined by several factors—general principles of good design, the size of available fuels, and the rather rigid requirements of fireplace thermodynamics.

Design: Good design requires proportions that fit a fireplace to a room and to a location in a room. A fireplace scaled too small or too large is *visually* disturbing. If it fails to supply adequate heat or gives too much heat for the size of the room, it is *physically* disturbing.

Although no formula has been devised to guarantee proper scale, you can usually rely on your own

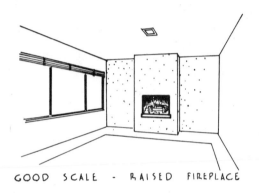

GOOD SCALE - RAISED FIREPLACE

good judgment. Proportions for a fireplace for a typical room may be helpful for a general guide. For a room 25 feet long, 12 feet wide, and 8½ feet high, a fireplace opening 30 to 36 inches in width is appropriate.

Fuel sizes: The conventional wood fuel sizes most readily obtainable in your area will have a bearing on the width of the fireplace opening. If you wish to use full-length 4-foot cordwood, for example, the proportions will differ from those of a fireplace suited to the use of half-length cordwood. Other common log lengths are 16 and 36 inches.

Thermodynamics: The heating action of a fireplace is principally that of radiation from the fire, the back wall, the sides, and the hearth. Because radiant heat travels in straight lines its range is limited.

To assure proper heating and to prevent smoking, it is necessary to follow closely the optimum dimensions that have been worked out by heating engineers from a careful study of fireplace operations. Too much variation from these dimensions will cause the fireplace to smoke and diminish the amount of heat it supplies. These dimensions are given in the chapter, "How to Build It Right."

WHAT MATERIALS ARE BEST?

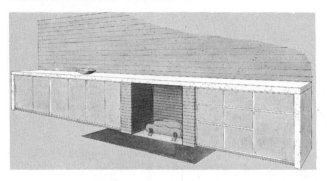

Fire and brick are peculiarly suited to each other. The warm tones of clay brick blend amiably with the orange of the flames and the ruby glow of the coals. Even when no fire is burning, the mellow bricks seem to suggest the promise of fire.

Bricks do not have to be laid in conventional courses. They may be laid up-ended or stacked to produce a strong vertical line; they may be laid in massive numbers to make a wall or partition; or, to break up space, they may even be set into the wall in the familiar patterns of the garden walk — herringbone, criss-cross, or basket weave.

The two types of bricks most generally used are known as common brick and face brick. Common is a porous, rough type, usually used for inner surfaces that do not show. Face brick is a hard-surfaced type, usually used for fireplace facings. If you plan to paint over the brickwork, use common bricks. Clay bricks are obtainable in a range of colors, running from red, through coral to buff.

Used bricks suggest another possibility. These bricks, with bits of mortar adhering to them, make a pleasant facing suitable for informal interiors. They are obtainable from wrecking companies or brickyards that specialize in handling them. Another variation is the long, thin Roman brick for producing strong horizontal lines.

In some types of homes, materials other than clay brick are often more suitable. The choice depends on simple preference, on the over-all plan of the house, or on the textures and colors needed for the decoration scheme in a particular room. In some situations, certain materials may be less expensive and more readily available than brick—such as the rock pile that came with your lot.

The choice is wide. You can select from materials almost as venerable as brick, notably, fieldstone and adobe. Other materials with a long fireplace tradition are tile, marble, and wood. For a very contemporary room, the need may be for a novel material such as corrugated iron, plastic sheeting, or roughened concrete.

Sim Bruce Richards, design; Ernest Braun, photo

Arch of dramatic fireplace unites the contrasting elements of wood and brick. Raised hearth extends to the wall out of sight on the left. Lighting is indirect, carried around the room in a valance paneled to match the mahogany walls

Fireplaces in wood walls

A fireplace fitted into a wood-paneled wall makes for a comfortable, easy-going room. In many of to-day's homes, the walls draw their color and tone from the exposed grain and texture of all-over wood paneling. And with most of the woods in popular favor, the traditional materials of fireplace construction make a pleasing, harmonious blend.

The colors of wood and masonry complement each other. The coral tones of common brick match the soft, warm browns of redwood and cedar; and buff-colored face bricks blend well with the straw tones of mahogany or pine veneers. Marble duplicates the watered-silk grain of birch plywood.

The texture of the fireplace facing may be designed either to harmonize or contrast with the wood panel-ing. A smooth-surfaced wood veneer often calls for a matching sheen of marble or burnished brass or copper, or it may require the jolting contrast of a rough stone or concrete facing to keep the over-all effect from becoming cold or over-elegant. Rough woodwork, like board and batten or knotty pine, provide an excellent casual background for a fire-place of dressed stone.

Johnson and Hawley, design

Steel framing permits this design of glass and wood above the fieldstone fireplace. Raised hearth is poured concrete

Otto Winkler, design; William Aplin, photo

Redwood, black marble, in scale with the large and simple living-room, create generous-sized, hospitable fireplace. Shares the same wall and chimney as den fireplace. Wood storage box behind cabinet at right is loaded from outside and also may be opened in den

Maynard Parker, photo

Dressed stone, laid in brick bond, gives pleasing rough effect to match the board and batten walls. Cattle-brand andirons

Gordon B. Kaufmann, design; Maynard Parker, photo

Masonry and wood happily combined in this fireplace wall: paneled with Port Orford cedar, stained light honey color

Mario Corbett, design; Philip Fein, photo

Above, left: Tooled gray concrete fireplace juts from wall to relieve severity of smooth hardwood veneer wall. Raised bricks fence hearth which continues to outer wall of room

James A. Lawrence, photo

Above, right: Black concrete of fireplace frame and hearth contrasts with living room walls of bleached mahogany veneer. Lamp black added to cement when cast resulted in high gloss

Paul Kirk, design; Dearborn-Massar, photo

Left: Fireplace frame and hearth are granite. Steel supports the hearth, a slab of stone. Paneling is Douglas fir

Chambers-Unthank, design; Tom Burns, Jr., photo

Below, left: A row of bricks defines the fireplace in this pine-paneled wall. Brick hearth is ½ inch above the floor

F. Harvey Slocumbe, design; Philip Fein, photo

Below, right: Curved masonry of dressed sandstone fireplace is topped with veneer. Fuel locker to right of fireplace may be loaded from outside. Mantel continues as top of bookcases

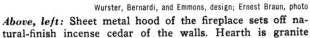

Wurster, Bernardi, and Emmons, design; Ernest Braun, photo

Above, left: Sheet metal hood of the fireplace sets off natural-finish incense cedar of the walls. Hearth is granite

Austin Pierpont, design; William Aplin, photo

Above, right: Dark tones of shadow box frame and Roman brick hearth accentuate salmon-colored facing, keep it from melting into redwood wall paneling. Magazine rack in wall

Frederick Monhoff, design; Julius Shulman, photo

Right: Well placed and scaled, this fireplace seems architecturally a part of the room, rather than something added on. Design utilizes three materials — wood, Roman bricks, tile

Charles Pearson, photo

Below, left: Black and white marble facing, combined with inset paneling, holds center of interest in formal living room. Two panels open for storage—one for firewood, one for games

Frederick Kline, design; Maynard Parker, photo

Below, right: Brick facing is banded with a strip of white pine that forms narrow mantel and side supports and ties in the fireplace with the white pine paneling used throughout room

Hart and Weiss, design; Ernest Braun, photo

Earth tones of the ceramic tile fireplace, board-on-board redwood walls combine to evoke an intimate mood in living room. Floor is green ceramic tile. Steel framing creates arch. Nine-foot ceiling helps to maintain room proportions

Jack De Longe, design; Maynard Parker, photo

Honey colored wall paneling is carried over fireplace facing, notched to provide a planting shelf. Opening is metal rimmed

Sewall Smith, design; Philip Fein, photo

Rock fireplace built into wall paneled with squares of lacquered redwood plywood. Upholstered bench covers storage

Harold Burket, design; Jerry Anson, photo

An intimate library fireplace is set flush with wall veneer. Facing and hearth are of Indiana limestone and floor is composed of cork tile. Built-ins are used exclusively in room

William Decker Holdredge, design; Miles Berne, photo

Small brick fireplace is set into masculine, pine paneled den. Musket, pistol, other relics give traditional touch to modern room. Brick in opening repeated in extended hearth

Otto Winkler, design; William Aplin, photo

Elevated fireplace framed in black marble is set into redwood wall. It shares the chimney with living room fireplace

Morley Baer, photo

Rough plank mantel blends with rough texture of the dressed sandstone fireplace and matches the pine walls and ceiling

John Lloyd Wright, design; Lynn Fayman, photo

Adobe brick has been turned bedside out to give an unusual rough texture to fireplace. Adobe hearth runs to the tile floor

Adobe for a Western touch

For a fireplace that looks at home in a Western ranch-style room, perhaps no material is more appropriate than adobe. Bricks made of adobe clay have been used in the Southwest for 175 years, ever since the Spaniards brought the ancient technique for making them to this far outpost of their empire. Out of the soil where they chose to build, they drew the raw material for their missions and haciendas, and for the fireplaces and ovens that warmed and served them.

In modern homes, adobe-brick fireplaces are most often found incorporated into an adobe wall, but occasionally the material is used just for a facing, in combination with rustic paneling. Where the fireplace is part of a wall, the adobe is usually plastered and painted; where it stands alone, it is often left in its natural, rich brown.

Adobe bricks are not notably fire-resistant, and, unless insulated with a hard-burned lining, they eventually crumble away from heat.

Blaine Drake, design; Julius Shulman, photo

Adobe corner fireplace breaks smoothness of a square living room and sets off kitchen alcove. Triangular hearth is sunken

David E. Horn, design; John Robinson, photo

Above: Fireplace is built around a metal form. Wood boxes are built on each side of the unit

Cliff May, design; Ernest Braun, photo

Right: Beamed ceiling combines with adobe in ranch house. Terrace and garden are outside

Jerry Anson, photo

Modest corner hearth proves adobe does not have to be used only in large-scale fireplaces

Hugh Comstock, design; Morley Baer, photo

Adobe of fireplace, timbers and ceiling rafters painted off-white. Wide fireplace opening framed with decorative brown tiles. Adobe brick floor, hearth

Eral Leek, design; Charles R. Pearson, photo

Mantel of rough 6x12-inch timber matches rugged character of fireplace. Stones, set in concrete, came from building site during excavation. Wooden mantel protected from fire with asbestos sheathed with copper. Hemlock floors and walls

Mantels and rooms

At one time, when the fireplace was depended upon to cook the family's meals, the mantel was one of its working parts. It served as a warming shelf and it kept pots, seasonings, and edibles off the floor, away from inquisitive pets and the swish of the mop.

Later on, when the fireplace had lost its pre-eminence in the kitchen and had been shifted to the living room, the mantel took on a refined and formal air. It became a display shelf for the family clock, art objects, candelabra.

In recent years, some designers have considered the mantel an unessential feature of fireplace design and have dispensed with it; but others have felt free to make imaginative use of it to tie the fireplace into the room design. No longer confined to the width of the facing, the mantel may be extended across an entire wall, joining bookshelves, counters, or storage cases, or merely carrying an architectural line. Or, the material and shape of the mantel itself may be used as a device to bring together the fireplace masonry and the surrounding wall surfacing.

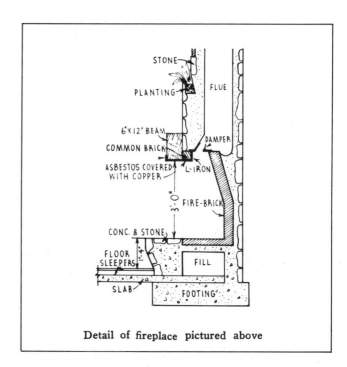

Detail of fireplace pictured above

Morley Baer, photo

Simple mantel, carried to wall, ties in the used-brick fireplace with the waxed pine walls

Hope Foote, design; Dearborn-Massar, photo

A simply decorated mantel ties the fireplace to the wall in this combination bedroom, office, and study. The face and hearth are ceramic tile

Marshall W. Perrow, design

Above: A long turquoise blue mantel joins the fireplace and bookcase, matches the horizontal line of Roman brick facing

Ulysses Floyd Rible, design; Woodcock, photo

Right: Long wood mantel accentuated by brass accessories and fireplace fender gives a traditional air to a modern room

Robbie Watson, design; Maynard Parker, photo

Wood paneling theme of walls repeated over fireplace. High mantelpiece balances. Brick facing painted to match walls

Jack De Longe, design; Maynard Parker, photo

Color of gold Roman brick fireplace repeated in wall and simple mantel. Wood storage locker at right. Opening 4' x 2'8

Ulysses Floyd Rible, design; Woodcock, photo

Elegant, carved mantel and side panels blended with modern materials: concrete lintel and Roman brick side facing

Philip Fein, photo

Hand carved walnut mantelpiece, from a pioneer home of 1872, looks at home against redwood paneling of present room

Lutah Maria Riggs, design; William Aplin, photo

Niches over fireplace show off art objects. Shelves for books utilize waste space created by slight extension of fireplace

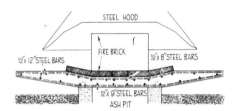

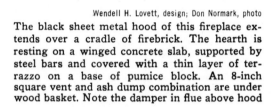

Wendell H. Lovett, design; Don Normark, photo

The black sheet metal hood of this fireplace extends over a cradle of firebrick. The hearth is resting on a winged concrete slab, supported by steel bars and covered with a thin layer of terrazzo on a base of pumice block. An 8-inch square vent and ash dump combination are under wood basket. Note the damper in flue above hood

Hearths — high and low

Basically, a hearth is simply a rectangle of masonry laid in front of the fireplace opening to protect wooden flooring from sparks and run-away logs and to push the floor back far enough so it will not be blistered or warped by the fire's heat.

With imaginative treatment, a hearth can do more than keep the house from catching fire. Floor-level hearths may be spread over a large area to create a fireplace room-within-a-room, or run as a band along a wall to tie the fireplace masonry into the room or into an adjacent room. Or, the hearth may be recessed below floor level to produce a fireplace sitting room.

A raised hearth brings the fireplace up to a more intimate height. This is a favored arrangement for small rooms, such as a den or study; or a dining room, kitchen, or game room, where it is awkward for persons seated at a table to see and enjoy a fire burning at floor level.

Raised hearths may be built up solidly from the floor, either flush with the wall or extended into the room. Often, such a hearth is designed with wings or extensions that can be used for work counters, benches, seats, or planting boxes.

Lockwood deForest, design; William Aplin, photo

Hearth, following wall angles, is cantilevered on steel frame, brings fireplace into room. Opening banded, studded in metal

Bassetti & Morse, design; Don Normark, photo

Double-chimneyed fireplace acts as room divider. Ample wood storage bin and open upper shelf

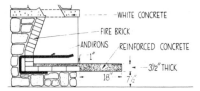

are shown to the left of face. The hearth is reinforced concrete 3⅓ inches thick, projects 1½ feet, and can be used as a seat. Levels of stone and mortar are broken by colored concrete slabs. The firebox is made of ten courses of firebrick

Jack White, photo

Long, clean line of fireplace hearth, gains interest from the recess for wood. Dressed stone blends with grayed plywood

Blaine Drake, design; Julius Shulman, photo

Hearth on two levels adds interest to brick fireplace. Grate, on upper hearth, may be used for barbecuing over coals

Cross section, looking from the end of the fireplace shown to right. The projecting concrete hearth cast integrally with the reinforced base

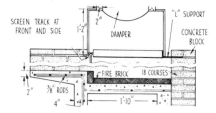

SCREEN TRACK AT FRONT AND SIDE
DAMPER
"L" SUPPORT
CONCRETE BLOCK
FIRE BRICK 18 COURSES
3/8" RODS
1'-2"
2"
2"
4"
1'-10"

Perry Johanson, design; Don Normark, photo

To preserve sense of openness and view, fireplace has a low silhouette. Set four feet from the glass wall, it has a planter behind. Hearth is a tumbled rock mosaic set in concrete. Flue and trim of the house are painted cream colored

Leonard Delano, photo

Hearthless fireplace, 18 inches off floor, built of native Oregon stone rimmed with concrete

Clifford McBride, design; Miles Berne, photo

This bold, hooded fireplace matches a large living room. The flagstone hearth is laid over brickwork. Wood storage cabinet built under the stairs

Above: Line of raised hearth is carried on both sides of the fireplace by bench-height ledge. The hooded opening, five feet high, is in proportion

Right: Raised hearth at left forms display space and a window seat that looks on a seascape. Open corner allows a view of the fire from hearth

High hearth facilitates use of this fireplace for cooking. Charcoal brazier is an iron pan set on two bricks in fireplace

Brick steps leading to platform seem structural part of fireplace. Steps form unusual hearth, are often used for seats

Richard Neutra, design; Julius Shulman, photo

Built-in bookshelves vary the theme of a mantel and do away with a symmetrical appearance of fireplace which may rigidly dominate the room. Fireplace serves as a wall between living and dining rooms. Sets off corner for moments of relaxation

Fireplaces and bookcases

From a design standpoint, bookcases make a good match for fireplaces. The horizontal sweep of the shelves serves to continue the mantel or hearth line around the wall. The depth of the shelving helps to bring the wall surface out to the level of the projecting masonry. Even the pattern formed by the spines of the books themselves seems to repeat the geometric design of the brickwork.

Bookcases and fireplaces may be combined in numberless ways. Narrow cabinets may be recessed in the masonry, shelving may be built to flank the fireplace or to run from the fireplace around one or two walls, or the shelves may be brought across the breast of the fireplace, above the mantel.

In most installations, the closeness of the books to the fireplace does no harm to them. Books are perishable commodities, however, and they can be damaged by too much dry heat. Where the shelves cross the chimney, if the fireplace is used continuously, the books may dry out and shed their bindings, unless they are rotated with books kept in cases not so close to the heat of the fire.

Darrow M. Watt, photo

Interest and utility were added to the fireplace in a subdivision home with 2 by 8-inch shelves and a plywood shelf

Bookcase is traffic divider masking a down stairway, rail on other side. In front, tile floor from hall flows past to merge with fireplace hearth. Bookcase lines carried through to form mantel strip. Wood storage cabinet to left of Roman brick unit

Fireplace with polished brass fender gives cozy feeling to this sitting room paneled with walnut veneer

Plywood treated with Belgium wax backs bookcases. Hand-tooled pine beams blend with dressed stone facing of flagstone hearth

Nello Zava, design; Jerry Anson, photo

Lines formed by the fireplace bricks, laid jack-on-jack, complement the verticle lines of books

Paul Kirk, design, Art Hupy, photo

Curved effect is created by the slanted bookcases flanking the fireplace. Native stone used in the masonry. High windows give view of treetops

John Morse, design; Art Hupy, photo

Bookshelves fill a solid part of the wall. Notice how the grille for an air-circulating fireplace is worked in with low-height shelves for albums. Niche for the painting is an architectural "frame." Raised hearth for extra seating

Buff, Straub, and Hensman, design; Ernest Braun, photo

Arrangement of the fireplace, bookshelf wall, and a built-in sofa creates a warm atmosphere. This concrete block fireplace acts as a room-divider, with the kitchen-dining area behind. The lighting cove was installed above the books because the dark bindings tend to soak up light. The Western theme is carried out by Indian pottery, rug and blanket

Charles Pearson, photo

Three rows of built-in bookcases top the fireplace wall of this room. Roman brick facing is set within shadow-box frame.

Ernest Braun, photo

Bookshelves and fireplace share a wall in this living room. Upper shelf is of cantilever type construction

Nello Zava, design; Jerry Anson, photo

Above: In this friendly corner, bookshelves cross over fireplace facing and form a wall between the living and dining room areas. Note the interesting triangular shaped hearth

Eral Leek, design; Charles Pearson, photo

Top, right: Open-sided fireplace built of two shades of Roman brick blends with the horizontal lines of the varnished cedar walls, bookshelves and built-ins. Fireplace angles into room

Jack White, photo

Right: Jog in the shelf and the band of bookcases carry out the horizontal lines. Built by the owner, the fireplace has a facing of native sandstone trimmed to regular shapes

Cliff May, design; Maynard Parker, photo

Below: Floor-to-rafter bookcases make for a studious corner near the fireplace. Facing of fireplace and flanking benches laid with 2x8-inch tiles. Mantel is formed by a single beam

Paul Thiry, design; Charles Pearson, photo

Below, right: Elevated fireplace in master bedroom overlooking a lake. Opening is banded and hooded with metal. Note the oversized mortar joints and the adjustable book cases

Fire with a view

Unusual see-through fireplace offers a view of the garden. Plants beyond are near eye-level and the fire seems almost outdoors. The glass at the rear is heat-resistant and stays clean for a long time because of the size of fireplace

Surrounded by glass, the "column" fireplace can look light and graceful or sturdy and sheltering

Living room fireplace in center of the window wall looks east on terrace. Burlap on the walls turned gold with age. Copper bucket for wood

Can you successfully blend two competitors for the center of attention like a fireplace and a picture window? That is a problem that many designers have to solve when they are selecting the location for a fireplace in a room with a window wall.

The solution depends on individual circumstances —the desires of the homeowners, the over-all plan for the room, or the structural limitations of the house itself. Some people do not like to mix the view with the hearth. They prefer to look at the scenery when they feel like it, or get away from it entirely and retire to the intimate, cave-like spell of the fire. Others enjoy the two together, relishing the contrast between a blustery scene in the garden and the blaze crackling on the hearth, or the harmony of flames indoors with the fire of autumn leaves outside.

Where the two elements are combined, furniture need not be arranged for two separate centers of interest, but can be oriented to the wall and fireplace the year around. Floor-to-ceiling pull draperies permit the view to be closed off when desired, thus changing the character of the room and transferring full emphasis to the fireplace.

Corner fireplace of brick sharply contrasts with window wall. Varying lines, raised portions and shelves all add interest

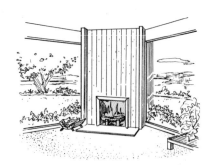

"Corner" fireplace is a variation of the column and allows a panoramic view through glass walls

Anshen and Allen, design; Mason Weymouth, photo

In small, subdivision house, the living room is oriented to the fireplace and walled front garden. Overhead beams link the garden to room. Glass contributes to the effect of spaciousness

Smith and Williams, design; Julius Shulman, photo

Fieldstone of the fireplace and hearth emphasizes the natural materials and complements wooded view beyond glass walls

Wurster, Bernardi, and Emmons, design; Darrow M. Watt, photo

At night, lighting on the terrace and the distant city lights cancel some of the after-dark blankness of a glass expanse

Glass above the fireplace is possible with a prefabricated or a patent flue, often outside room

George T. Rockrise, design; Ernest Braun, photo

Furniture can be arranged around the fireplace, yet take advantage of the landscape. Room also open to the sky, with a frosted glass skylight so fireplace is never silhouetted by the glare

Robert J. Peterson, design; Charles R. Pearson, photo

Small-scaled fireplace, broad glass wall, and the terrace flush with the concrete slab floor bring garden into room

William Wallace Reid, design; William Aplin, photo

Glass above the storage cabinets and fireplace gives roof floating look. Bulk of the fireplace is outside the wall

Anshen and Allen, design; Morley Baer, photo

Built of river rocks, the fireplace forms an artificial cave, contrasting with the openness of the glass walls. The black sheet metal hood rests on firebrick. A skylight over the storage bin admits diffused light and is lit in the evening

Jerry Anson, photo

Indoor plant box, large expanse of glass, link outdoor and indoor living room. Painted bricks laid vertically continue sweep of the draperies. Brick work continues behind plant box. Upper section of fireplace extends over opening

Paul Thiry, design; Charles Pearson, photo

Open fire and view through glass wall are enjoyed at same time in this room. High brick shelf for display of brass, copper. Two-sided corner opening adds cheerfulness. Angle of raised hearth forms resting place for fire tools. An iron post supports the lintel

Store the wood nearby

Jack Stafford, design; Carroll Calkins, photo

Electric motor in attic pulls up wood in a steel lift from the garage below the house

A hungry fireplace can consume several armloads of fuel in the course of a long evening. A busy firetender comes to appreciate the convenience of having ample wood nearby, so he doesn't have to lug it in from the garage or struggle with it up the basement stairs any oftener than absolutely necessary.

There are many practical ways to provide for fuel storage in a fireplace plan. Most convenient arrangement is a fireside locker with a door that opens outside or into the garage. This permits the wood supply to be stacked in place without tramping winter mud through the house, or leaving a trail of bark, pitch, splinters, or dropped logs. Inside the room, the wood cabinet itself can easily be integrated with the fireplace and wall design. The door can be balanced with other living room cabinets or concealed in wood paneling.

Sometimes, it is desirable frankly to expose the pile of wood, stacked in a recess or under a cantilevered hearth, to display the promise of long, enjoyable fires.

A bin for wood storage is provided under this upholstered fireplace seat. A removable tray for ashes eases fireplace cleaning

Photo and sketch show ingenious way to provide wood from outside a one-level house. Dolly loads in carport, rolls through opening in the wall into built-in cabinet near fire

Hoist below the fireside wood box brings firewood up from the basement. Lid of wood box could also be used as seat

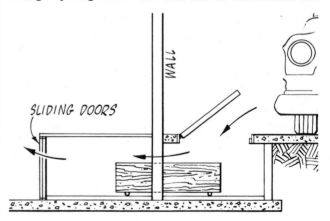

SLIDING DOORS

WALL

George R. Bartholick, design; Carroll Calkins, photo

Door of cabinet (in photo at right) opens to an outside wood box. The shelf is used for papers, gloves and matches

Fireplace area is unified by extended hearth, horizontal line from top of the wood storage bin through brick shelf

Norris Gaddis, design; Carroll Calkins, photo

Door to wood storage bin blends in with the plaster wall. The fireplace facing is Roman brick with the rough side out

Wood for the fireplace shown at left is stored outside on an 8-foot shelf. Note back of the door next to fireplace

Lutah Maria Riggs, design; Maynard Parker, photo

Firewood is always at hand, yet never in the way, in this decorative storage recess. Inner hearth is made of brick

J. R. Davidson, design; William Aplin, photo

Roman brick counter forms a sturdy wood storage cabinet and carries out horizontal lines of this interesting fireplace unit

W. S. Hayden, design; Carroll Calkins, photo

Roman brick fireplace has wood storage built into the masonry. Loading is through a door from back of the recess

Young and Richardson, design; Charles Pearson, photo

Wood storage bin occupies right half of long, raised fireplace unit, and shares brass fire curtain with the fireplace

George Badger, design; Jerry Anson, photo

Fireplaces as partitions

By expanding the masonry on each side of a fireplace, it is relatively easy to stretch it into a small wall. Set it down inside the house, away from the outside wall, and, presto, it becomes a partition.

Fireplace partitions are useful for separating living room and hall, living room and dining room. The depth of the masonry needed for the fireplace's inner workings makes the wall deep enough for use as a storage wall. Cabinets or closets may be fitted into the brickwork on either side of the wall; the reverse side may also house a fireplace in another room, such as a den or a kitchen-dining room combination.

As evident from the samples that follow, a fireplace partition does not have to fill to ceiling height. A counter-height fireplace, with ceramic or enameled steel flues, makes an arresting divider between living and dining rooms.

Top: Freestanding, acting as partition, fireplace is feature of room. Will accept any furniture grouping mood suggests

Francis Joseph McCarthy, design; Roger Sturtevant, photo

Right: Living-dining partition, storage in other side. Oak plywood stained black. Flues, cement frame painted ivy green

Harwell Harris, design; Maynard Parker, photo

Fireplace forms a corner partition where the hall leads into kitchen (left) and bedroom. A cabinet between fireplace and bookshelves holds a record player and radio. Sheet metal hood rises to a high ceiling with clerestory windows

Paul Thiry and John Sproule, design;
Charles Pearson, photo

Extension of fireplace wall into partition, shields the living room from hallway traffic. Other side of wall is used for storage. Cabinets shown at this end hold card tables. Wall broken for more light

Gregory Ain, design; Julius Shulman, photo

Fireplace forms wall between hall stairwell and living room. Has inviting airy expanse in good proportion to living room. Mantel trough for indirect lighting. Planter in brickwork and at stair head

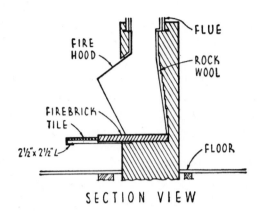

FIRE HOOD

FLUE

ROCK WOOL

FIREBRICK TILE

2½" × 2½" L

FLOOR

SECTION VIEW

Francis Joseph McCarthy, design; Ernest Braun, photo

Above: Brick fireplace was built around a patent form and separates the living and dining areas in this cabin. One flue leads to a barbecue below. Rocks-in-concrete hearth

Paul Kirk, design; P. A. Dearborn, photo

Right: Fireplace forms a partition that screens hall into bedroom. Grille at top of the fireplace wall admits heat from the furnace. Roman brick with a common brick hearth

Gregory Ain, design; Philip Fein, photo

Below: Circular inset in fireplace of faced brick is for radio speaker. Indirect lighting is hidden behind top of brickwork. In back of fireplace is a wood storage cabinet

Francis Joseph McCarthy, design; Roger Sturtevant, photo

Below, right: Top of fireplace creates a wide mantel that provides a serving counter for the dining room. Exposed flues, hearth, and the corrugated cement facing are mauve

Cliff May, design; Julius Shulman, photo

A dark brown ceramic flying goat, with gray-green glaze, decorates this corner fireplace with brick mantel and hearth.

Master bedroom takes on living room quality with sliding glass doors. Fireplace blends, becomes incidental part of room

Accent with ornamentation

One way to make a fireplace the dominant feature of a room is to combine a simply-designed facing with a rich, ornamental device placed above the mantel.

When the fire is burning, the play of the flames accentuates the plainly-treated opening, bringing it into equality with the decoration. When no fire is burning, the ornament holds the center of attention, drawing the eye away from the dead ashes on the hearth.

For a long time, the accepted art form to place above the mantel was an oil painting of a landscape or a grim member of the family tree. This is still an excellent device, but, as the photographs show, there are fresher choices at hand.

It could be a ceramic beast of mythological ancestry, a patined weathervane from an antique shop or grandfather's barn, a mosaic of tile or pebbles, a tinplate devil's mask, or a free-form design shaped from copper tubing. It could be a literary or religious tale, told in fresco. It might be a chip-carved design in a redwood mantel or lintel beam.

McFarland-Bonsall, design; Douglas M. Simmonds, photo

Den fireplace with used brick hearth is framed by Mexican tiles set into the plaster. Walls and cabinets are beige

Henry Hill, design

At right, taffy-colored Mexican onyx chips, set in concrete squares, form an unusual facing for this fireplace. Shown above are textures possible in stone and concrete: rough, semi-smooth or tumbled, semi-polished, and highly polished

Jerry Anson, photo

Stuffed ducks decorate paneled study wall. Door at right holds built-in typewriter-desk which is ready for use as door opens

Dearborn-Massar, photo

Striking wood sculpture contrasts with the plain face of used-brick fireplace. The hearth and floor are red brick

Marshall W. Perrow, design; Hugh N. Stratford, photo

Glass on three sides of the fireplace minimizes light contrast from the outside. Door leads to outside wood storage

Brighten a corner

On first thought, a corner might seem to be an off-hand spot to locate a fireplace. Yet, far from being an awkward or retiring site for a hearth, a corner, if properly utilized, may be made to seem a natural and fitting location for a fireplace.

In fact, a corner fireplace may have considerable dramatic impact, particularly if it is designed to angle across the corner and break up the rectangular shape of the room.

A corner has some advantages over a flat wall as a place to put the fireplace. Everyone can see and enjoy the fire burning on a corner hearth, because there are no blind spots at each side of the fireplace. Benches and couches, placed against the walls that fan out from a corner, are all within the flames' light and circle of warmth.

Richard Massen and Roland D. Green, design; Julius Shulman, photo

Center, right: Raised hearth, frankness, honesty invite comradeship. Masonry wall takes over important corner here

Marjorie Wintermute, design

Below, right: Wire-cut common brick set in two patterns to form corner between indoor, outdoor rooms. Sliding glass wall

Henrik Bull, design

Above: In low-ceilinged room, the fireplace heats an entire cabin from the corner. Sheet metal hood makes an effective heat conductor. High hearth is framed by concrete blocks

Chiarelli & Kirk, design; Charles R. Pearson, photo

Above, right: Tall column flanking the Roman brick fireplace echoes the lines of vertical cedar in ceiling and wall. Couch against the window opens into an extra bed

John Lautner, design; Jerry Anson, photo

Right: This corner fireplace is in keeping with the cave-like quality of living room alcove. Long, brick seat runs into fireplace, serves as secondary inner hearth. Brick table pedestals

Jon Konigshofer, design; Morley Baer, photo

Below, left: A corner of used bricks contains a raised fireplace with wide hearth cushioned for leisure moments. Barbecue in patio shares common chimney with fireplace in this room

Richard Fish, photo

Below, right: Remodeled porch has painted brick fireplace that uses the living room fireplace chimney. Paneling is pine, painted gray. Seating at corners of the high hearth

Robert Lym, Jr., design; Ernest Braun, photo

Fireplace wall extends across living room. The foam rubber pads on the hearth, at either side of fireplace, can sleep guests

The whole wall a fireplace

When the plans call for a dominating fireplace—one that unquestionably holds the center of attention in a living room—a proven way to achieve this effect is to design the fireplace into a masonry wall so it looks as if the wall itself were an enlargement of the fireplace facing.

A large expanse of masonry, however, may give a monotonous or oppressive effect if it is not treated with subtlety. The photographs that follow show some of the ways of avoiding the deadening effect of solid masonry.

Variations in pattern help. The brickwork may be laid in basket-weave pattern, stacked up like dollars, or mortared with wide joints to create a stronger grid of white running through the masonry. A wall of Roman brick tends to appear lighter in tone than one of common brick—even though they contain the same amount of mortar—because of the strong horizontal lines formed by the joints. Carefully fitted stonework provides an interesting, rugged design.

Color can be kept from a monotone by mingling bricks of varying shades or by utilizing used bricks with their softening patches of old mortar.

A fireplace wall, if properly designed, may be used as a bearing wall—with approval from the City Hall.

Sim Bruce Richards, design; John Hartley, photo

Hood hangs like ornament on used-brick wall. Open three sides, fireplace has recessed fire to halt blowing ashes

Victor Wandmayer, design; Philip Fein, photo

Above, left: Fireplace-wall of Roman brick laid "jack-on-jack" continues from living room into patio. Plant box along wall base brings garden into room. Glass wall framed in redwood

Carnie Generaux, design; Maynard Parker, photo

Above, right: Painted Roman bricks around fireplace opening contrast with mauve tone of upper brickwork, living room walls and mantel. Fireplace accessories in brass and copper

Jack Buchter, design; Howard B. Hoffman, photo

Right: Roman brick fireplace and bookshelves are deftly tied together with a continuation of the shelf to form a mantel frame. The walls extend outside to enclosed patio

Ellis Jacobs, design; Clyde Childress, photo

Below, left: Wall, fireplace, and bench are all of concrete block. Note use of six protruding blocks. Five translucent glass blocks replace concrete and admit outdoor light

Joseph Allen Stein, design; Ernest Braun, photo

Below, right: Brick surrounding fireplace has jack-on-jack design, while band running across the top and down one side is a combination of "stretchers," protruding "headers"

Robert B. Price, design; Charles R. Pearson, photo

White plaster fireplace hood is mounted on a red brick wall extending past a glass wall to terrace. Hearth for seating

Paul Thiry, design; Art Hupy, photo

Wall of gray-green granite blocks gathered by owners, then trimmed, extends past bookcase to the entry at the right

John Rohrer, design; Howard Staples, photo

Fireplace-wall of hollow tile has mantel formed of a brass strip embedded in masonry; storage rack of black iron bars

Mark Voris, design; Maynard L. Parker, photo

Firewall helps to divide the room into three areas. Closets are built into the firewall. Table was an artist's modeling stand

Pleasing contrast of brick and dressed flagstones. Sand-mold bricks in hearth match rough texture of stone in fireplace

Fireplace-wall of carefully fitted stonework helps to bring together the outdoor and indoor living rooms of this house

Sunken hearth sets fireplace apart from rest of room. Brick pattern and mass dominate but become structural part of room

Red of the bricks accents soft hues of fieldstone wall in small living room. Sliding glass doors open to the garden

Jack Burkens, photo

Raised kitchen barbecue-fireplace is backed up against living room fireplace at right, shares chimney. Barbecue grill can be set at two levels to take full advantage of burning coals

Living room fireplace is built around corner to form kitchen barbecue at left. Same mantel design used on two fireplaces relates them to each other. Hearth material also is the same

Two-for-one

To get added value from your fireplace masonry, you can build two fireplaces back to back. Also, you can eliminate the back of the firebox to get a double view of the fire, or you can widen the view by opening the fireplace on two or three sides.

If planned with restraint, the back-to-back fireplace may often lead to economies in construction because the two fireplaces get by with only one foundation and a single chimney. However, any saving over separate fireplaces may be canceled out if the combination involves intricate bricklaying, such as might be needed in a triangular layout. It should be noted that when two fireplaces use the same chimney, each should have its own flue.

When the central living room fireplace is built into an inside wall, the extra fireplace in back of it may be fitted into the dining room or kitchen, a study, or even a bedroom. When the principal fireplace is fitted into an outside wall, an outdoor fireplace or barbecue may be incorporated into the exposed masonry.

There are several practical ways for laying out a back-to-back combination. The two fireplaces at the top of this page are angled across the corner of each room in this fashion:

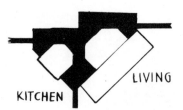

Another successful method involves arranging the opposing fireplaces in a straight line in this manner:

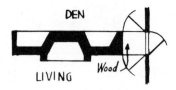

One advantage of this particular plan is that it makes provision for storage space, including a very handy wood cupboard. These features are easier to work into a partition wall of this type than into a corner with its odd irregular angles.

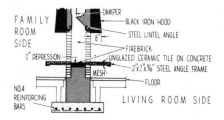

Robert B. Price, design; Dearborn-Massar, photo

Fireplace wall, forming divider between the living room and the family room, is at right angles to windows, so that the effect of cross-draft is minimized. As the sketch shows, tile-clad concrete slab forms hearth locked into the chimney masonry. Acoustical ceiling and throw rugs reduce noise. Painted brick wall has a metal hood

MULTI-FACED FIREPLACES

To emphasize a contemporary setting—and in addition to get a better view of your fire—you can open a fireplace on two or three sides. The projecting-corner fireplace (shown on page 54, upper right) is typical.

Still another method of increasing the view of your fire is to construct a standard fireplace—but leave out the reflecting back wall. The opening thus formed becomes the second fireplace, serving another room.

But with these fireplaces go special engineering problems that usually add to the cost. They offer less protection from cross-drafts in the room and require more generous flues and dampers. Particularly difficult are the three-sided fireplace and the see-through fireplace, such as the one shown at the upper left of this page.

Flue-size. As with the conventional fireplace, flue size depends upon the area of the fireplace opening. However, you must measure the *total* area of all faces. The minimum area necessary for your flue will be $\frac{1}{12}$ of the fireplace opening area if you have a round flue, $\frac{1}{10}$ if you have a rectangular one, and $\frac{1}{8}$ if your flue is un-

Dorothy Wintermute, design; B. J. Allen, photo

Doors of fire-resistant glass on the den side of this two-way fireplace are used to close fireplace and improve draft

Fireplace can be seen from at least three sides. The design uses Roman brick columns and raised concrete hearth

This three-sided fireplace is brick framed in steel. The dining area and kitchen share the view from the window wall

lined. Some experts recommend making the flue area one size larger than minimum.

Damper. Because more air enters your fireplace, you may also need a larger damper to accommodate the

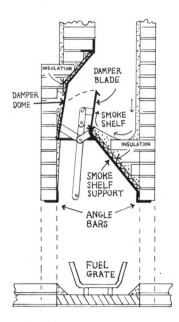

High damper is manufactured expressly for see-through and other multiple opening fireplaces. Smoke shelf is built in

greater volume of combustion gases. With a three-sided fireplace, it is wise to set the smoke chamber back, so that it is not directly above the damper; otherwise, you run the risk of a downdraft blowing smoke into the room.

Some manufacturers offer dampers specially designed for these fireplaces.

Drafts. Air currents are tricky, and before you put in a multi-faced fireplace, you may wish to consult an architect or fireplace designer. But some pointers may be helpful.

The slightest turbulence in the air may cause the fire to pull to one side and discharge smoke into the room. In general, it is safest to install the fireplace where its openings are not in the paths between doors and windows.

Lowering the firepit below the level of the opening will help prevent ashes blowing into the room. Some builders recommend a fan in the flue, to insure proper air flow up the chimney; but with a fan, you won't get much benefit from the fire's heat.

Glass doors on one side of a see-through fireplace will operate like a back wall and thus make it perform like a conventional fireplace. Glass should be a special, heat-resistant type. Thickness depends upon size of opening. Setting the glass in hinged frames facilitates fire-tending.

Fireplace with copper hood gives feeling of an open camp-fire. It is designed so that large groups can sit by the

W. F. Severin, design; Carroll Calkins, photo

fire without crowding, and separates bookcase corner from the main traffic flow. The brick hearth has steel support

Freestanding fireplaces

Among designers and builders, the free-standing fire-place is a subject of sharp disagreement. For those who like their fires dramatized, this modern adaptation of the primitive open cooking fire accents the hearth in striking fashion and quite literally holds the center of attention. Yet many experts feel that it is unpredictable.

The larger the fireplace opening, the greater draft is necessary to keep the fire burning properly. But a fire is extremely sensitive to movements in the air—opening a nearby door or window, even walking past the fire too rapidly, may cause it to pull to one side and throw smoke into the room.

Therefore, the main problem is to supply enough draft to keep the free-standing fireplace from smoking, and at the same time to prevent air currents from de-flecting smoke into the room. (See also pages 53–54.)

Some experts recommend that air be piped directly from outside the house to the fire. You can set a cold-air register, the kind used for air-circulating furnaces, be-side the hearth and run a pipe under the floor directly through to the side of the house. Or you can install the register in the firepit itself.

Another way to insure that combustion gases are carried off properly is to put in a fan. Best place for the fan is near the top of the flue.

THE METAL HOOD

A metal hood has the advantage of needing no corner supports. If it is heavy, it may require substantial flash-ing, though, and plenty of roof support to prevent side

place opening. If anything, err on the side of too much rather than too little flue area. Also, the higher the flue, the greater the draft will be.

To get the width of the fireplace opening, measure the circumference of the hood at its mouth. Height is the distance from the rim of the hood to a point level with the fireplace opening.

SPECIAL PRECAUTIONS

As with the conventional fireplace, the free-standing

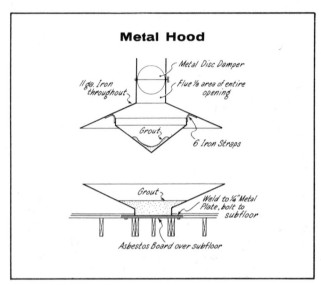

John Fisher, design; Art Hupy, photo

Lanai fireplace and floor are Arizona flagstone. Fan in the flue keeps drafts balanced when sliding doors are open

sway. In addition, the metal hood is a good heat conductor. (See pages 58–63.)

It is wise to extend the rim of the hood well beyond the circumference of the firepit and to allow at least a 35-degree slope. Many builders advise a damper and smoke shelf or baffle in the flue. Also, a flue cap can help stop downdrafts.

FLUE AREA

Flue area should be about ⅛ the area of the fire-

fireplace needs an outer hearth to catch falling sparks. A screen is also advisable. Check with your building inspector for local regulations.

A metal firebox that isn't insulated can become hot enough during the course of an evening's fire to cause memorable burns. Also, it is a good idea to place your firebox at least 3 feet from walls, windows, and seating arrangements. If your draft comes from a window or door, anyone sitting in its path may feel the coldness of the blast.

Metal, conical firepit

Metal pipes support masonry

Hood with freestanding wall

Tom Burns, Jr., photo

One answer to smoke problem is this adjustable galvanized hood. It drops down for starting fire and to contain the coals at night. The rail is copper pipe. Expanded shale blocks in firepit. Traffic lane around the fireplace is laid with linoleum. Combination of draperies and bamboo screens over the windows help cut glare

William F. Hempel, design; Ernest Braun, photo

Brick-based fireplace in this beach house has a copper hood with wide metal chimney. Lowered firepit gives protection from cross drafts. The fireplace can warm the entire living room, but additional heating is supplied. Draperies are sunfast. Asphalt tile floor, plywood walls, and hard finish upholstery defy sun, sand, and water

Wilkins and Ellison, design; Clyde Childress, photo

Sole source of heat in cabin is the fireplace. For a feeling of lightness, the hood is suspended from the high roof and radiates heat all the way up. Steps down to the sunken recess, focus of living area, are used for seating. Sand piled high in brazier insulates floor from heat. Note pulley kerosene lamp hanging next to the hood

Morley Baer, photo

Living room fireplace of simple elements — hearth, hood, brick wall — set against redwood panels. Firebox floor enclosed

Hoods: dramatic and efficient

A metal hood provides a dramatic but efficient feature for a modern fireplace. But it can serve more than strictly decorative ends: it can increase the effectiveness of the fireplace by radiating heat when it is warmed up, and the heat of the metal encourages greater air circulation up the flue.

The lustre of the bright metal enhances a room that takes its tone from the natural texture, color, and grain of the materials built into it. A hood may be fashioned of copper, polished bright, left a warm flame red, or oxidized green. It may be made of sheet metal with antique finish; a white metal such as aluminum or stainless steel; or steel plate, finished a charcoal black to contrast with red brickwork. Texture or pattern may be added by sandblasting, hammering, polishing, etching, or tool marking.

Often, a hooded fireplace is simpler to build than a masonry type, because it sometimes permits elimination of heavy chimney work and foundation masonry. Some localities permit a simple brick hearth and firewall, adequate for a hooded outlet, to be built right over the flooring. Metal hoods and flues call for the skilled hand of a master metalworker.

Jackson and Scott, design; Maynard Parker, photo

Fireplace forming living room wall, built of volcanic granite, with bright copper hood. Wood stored below curved hearth

Gordon Drake, design; Morley Baer, photo

Brick firewall with corner opening, shining copper hood, redwood paneling brings room to life. Business end of hearth of firebrick

Maynard Parker, photo

Fireplace front takes form of hood. Banded by column of bricks, bookshelves on either side. Raised brick hearth

Fred Langhorst, design; Ernest Braun, photo

Hood of concrete on brick corner wall. Dry mix troweled on wooden form, straw yellow color in topping

Mario Corbett, design; Ernest Braun, photo

Clean-lined fireplace and copper hood angle out to favor both the kitchen and large living-dining area. Hearth follows line of hood

Pietro Belluschi, design; Ron Partridge, photo

Copper hood radiates heat and serves as attractive cover for brick and concrete fireplace flue extending from ceiling to within few inches of bottom of hood. End and front backed with asbestos paper. Hood and panel prefabricated and fitted over chimney. Bottom of hood 42 inches above firebed which is 18 inches above floor. Hearth 16 feet long. Plan below

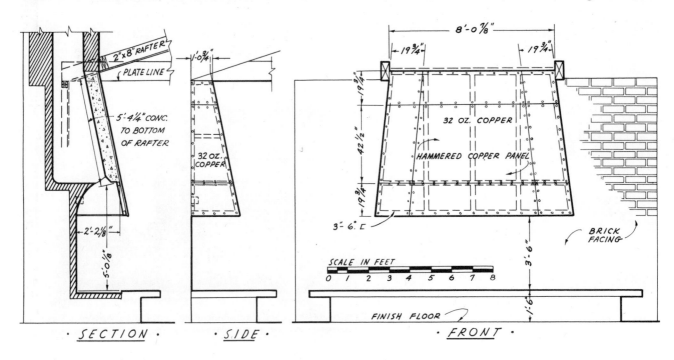

Vladimir Ossipoff, design; R. Wenkam, photo

Library fireplace has a plaster hood over a frame that covers an insulated, galvanized iron flue. Firebrick, stone in bed

Russell Forester, design; Morley Baer, photo

Three-sided fireplace, copper hood, opens to the bedroom, living room, and dining room. Wood stored under the hearth

Richard Lytel, design; Charles Pearson, photo

Fireplace grouping creates room within room. Studded metal hood tops facing of Roman brick with intimate raised hearth

William Corlett, design

Steel hood contrasts with the concrete blocks, laid jack-on-jack, of the wall. The wide, raised hearth is concrete

George Kosmak, design; Ernest Braun, photo

Jerry Anson, photo

This small fireplace, made of bricks and terrazzo slabs, has a metal hood. Andiron also serves as a grate. Patent flue

Copper hood, edged with brass, is set against firewall of firebrick. Flue consists of pipe inserted in hole cut through wall

Charles Pearson, photo

This fireplace extends into living room, is two feet above floor. Corner seat at fireplace right above wood storage bin.

Brick of fireplace continues around corner, forms bar. Metal hood made of steel traffic plate. Built-ins of combed plywood

Variation of metal hood, facing made of copper strips welded together with V-seams. Vertical seams echo Roman brickwork

Above: Copper hood and copper-covered flue cover a firebox attached to a two-brick thick firewall. Hood design scored on back side. Chimney section has galvanized inner flue inside copper, 1-inch air space between. Gas igniter in hearth

Right: Hammered copper hood. Construction is simple: angle iron frame made first. Sheet metal riveted and welded to frame, copper next with ½ inch asbestos between. Angle irons secured to brick with 6-inch lag screws. Terra cotta flues covered with copper tube, air space left open between

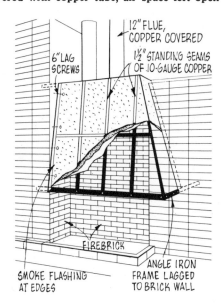

H. J. Williams, design; Julius Shulman, photo

Grate simply rests in a bed of sand. Valve at the right in the sand controls gas log lighter. The hood is low, to catch smoke

Metal fireplaces

A few decades ago, when all fireplaces were important sources of heat, you were likely to find small metal fireplaces in almost any room of the house. Today, although central heating has pretty well supplanted fireplace heating, many home owners are rediscovering the metal fireplace and some of its advantages.

Any well-designed model is at least as efficient as a masonry fireplace. Under normal conditions, it should not smoke, and it should draw well because metal warms up faster than stone. Also, a metal fireplace radiates heat from the sides and hood, so that even a small, compact version can be a major heat source for a room or an entire cabin.

Often, you can save a great deal of labor and expense by installing a metal instead of a masonry fireplace—especially when you remodel. While the house is being built, a masonry fireplace will cost little, if anything, more to put in. If you install the masonry fireplace later,

Darrow M. Watt, photo

Franklin stove makes a good metal fireplace. The hearth is concrete blocks. Metal back plate has air space behind it

though, you will usually run into additional costs, because a heavy concrete foundation must be laid, walls torn open, and the mortar mess kept under control.

If you have a handyman's bent, you can install a metal fireplace yourself, often in one day. A foundation is seldom needed. The fireplace moves in like an appliance. Most models, but not all, require some simple type of hearth. Biggest part of the job will be cutting a hole through the ceiling and roof, then assembling the patent or prefabricated flue there.

In remote places where an expert fireplace mason is not available, you can generally count on any good manufactured model to perform well under normal conditions. Also, metal fireplaces come in such a variety of designs that you can find one suitable to almost any setting. You can also buy a prefabricated firebox and face it with masonry.

Unless the fireplace hooks into an existing flue, you may want to install one of two types of chimney: the prefabricated or the patent chimney. You buy the prefabricated chimney in sections, usually consisting of an inner and an outer steel pipe separated by insulating material. The sections twist-lock together, so that no mortar is needed. Each manufacturer also provides a variety of attachments.

Be sure to check with your building inspector before installing a metal fireplace or patent chimney. Many

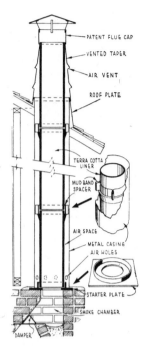

PATENT CHIMNEY

municipalities follow the Uniform Building Code, which approves some metal fireplaces but not all. If you install a metal stack inside a wall, you will probably have to maintain a minimum distance from combustibles and ventilate the collar that joins the stack to the wall.

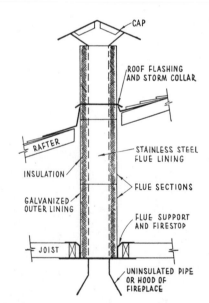

PREFABRICATED CHIMNEY

The patent chimney is a terra cotta flue liner surrounded by an incombustible metal casing. The casing may be left exposed, sheathed in another decorative metal sleeve, or concealed inside the walls of the structure.

George Kosmak, design; Ernest Braun, photo
Fireplace fits into a window alcove. Hearth is made of brick laid in mortar over chicken wire nailed to the floor

Wendell Lovett, design; Dearborn-Massar, photo

Above: Prefabricated fireplace is bright red, to go with cheerful colors in the living room. Made of sheet metal, it comes with the screen. Here it rests on a concrete base

George Kosmak, design; Glenn Christiansen, photo

Right: Fireplace hangs from the ceiling of a cabin, its flue giving extra heat. A sphere is an efficient shape because it distributes the heat evenly and the metal doesn't distort

Stephen Oyakawa, design; R. Wenkam, photo

Below, left and right: Double fireplace is used either indoors or out. Firebox is a heavy iron bowl, hood a copper cone, both centered in a concrete block wall. Hood has a metal damper to close off one side when the other is used

Ernest Braun, photo

Above, left: The Ornate facing of this cast-iron fireplace sets off the brick wall. It could also be used free standing

George Kosmak, design; Gerald Ratto, photo

Above, right: This fireplace hangs from the wall and hooks to flue openings for kitchen range, heater, in older homes

John Konigshofer, design; Morley Baer, photo

Right: Fireplace sets in a corner. The flue is lined with terra cotta. Asbestos is between masonry, walls, and floor

C. W. Smith, design

Below, left: Combination fireplace and shelving makes room divider. Unit is made of steel and assembles without bolts

Julius Shulman, photo

Below, right: This eighteenth-century Flemish fireplace is set with white tiles. The hearth can be flush with floor

Concrete block fireplace built around air circulating shell. Outlets in mantel. Cold air intake, left, other in woodbox

Freestanding fireplace in mountain cabin. Cold air intake through slots in base, hot air outlet through brick grating

The fireplace as furnace

How can you be sure that your fireplace won't smoke? The best answer is a prefabricated metal fireplace form. How can you make a fireplace heat a room? Install a heat-circulating unit.

The heat-circulating unit is designed to circulate heat through a room. It does this by heating air in strategically located metal ducts and returning the warmed air to the room. The air ducts can be extended into other rooms so that the fireplace can dis-

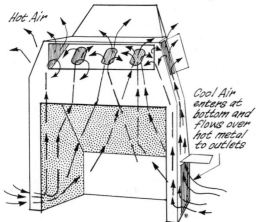

tribute heat to rooms at the sides or in back of it or upstairs. This type often is called a modified fireplace. In operation, modified fireplaces overcome several deficiencies of the standard fireplace. All fireplaces, of course, must draw air in order for the fire

to burn. This causes uncomfortable drafts and temperature variations in a room since the air at floor level drawn toward the fire is colder than air at shoulder height. In the standard fireplace, after the

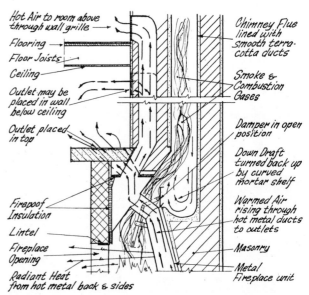

air has warmed most of it disappears up the chimney.

The modified fireplace puts the heated air to work warming the room. It draws cool air to inlets placed at low levels, heats the air and releases it through outlets placed where desired.

To improve circulation further, an electric ventilating fan can be placed in the pipe, either at the cool air inlet or heated air outlet. A fan is essential for

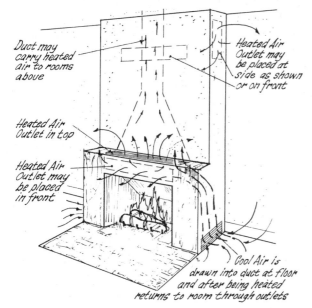

Duct may carry heated air to rooms above

Heated Air Outlet may be placed at side as shown or on front

Heated Air Outlet in top

Heated Air Outlet may be placed in front

Cool Air is drawn into duct at floor and after being heated returns to room through outlets

circulating units if the warm air pipe rises at less than 3 inches for each foot on the horizontal. Manufacturers specify fans that suit their units, and some make grilles with the fan built in.

Tests show that these units have distributed warm air to corners of the room which were cold when a non-circulating fireplace was in use. Temperatures of

over 200 degrees have been recorded at outlets. This increased heating efficiency does not mean circulating units can replace central heating furnaces in colder regions.

LOCATION OF INLETS

There are two ways of installing cool-air inlets for recirculating units. The air intakes may be located outdoors to draw in fresh air, or they may be placed inside the house, where they suck in indoor air at room temperature. In some localities, the indoor inlet

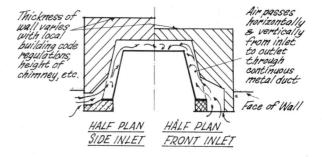

Thickness of wall varies with local building code regulations, height of chimney, etc.

Air passes horizontally & vertically from inlet to outlet through continuous metal duct

Face of Wall

HALF PLAN SIDE INLET   HALF PLAN FRONT INLET

may be found to be more efficient, because in extremely cold weather, air drawn in from outdoors may not become sufficiently heated before it is discharged into the room.

Indoor Inlets: When the inlets are installed indoors, they are placed at floor level to draw in the cool air that settles to the floor.

Terry & Moore, design; Dearborn-Massar, photo

Corner fireplace has ducts at the side. Cupboard under the hearth holds kindling. Foam rubber on built-in platform

Ted Rand, design; Charles R. Pearson, photo

Air circulating ducts open in facing of simple fireplace in studio-living room. Walls and ceiling are of combed plywood

Inlets may be exposed on the front or side of the fireplace facing, their openings covered with metal, brick, or stone grilles. Those with tiny, closely spaced horizontal fins are pleasing in appearance. If exposed grilles and openings displease you, conceal inlets in the hearth overhang.

If the fireplace is in the end wall of a very long, narrow room, use a ventilating fan to increase the heating action of the recirculating unit. Locate cool-air inlets in the opposite end wall. Install fans in these to speed flow of cold air toward the fireplace. Connect the inlet with the fireplace by an inlet pipe. The fireplace manufacturer will give you full specifications. You can do this also with a fireplace located in the side wall.

Fresh-air Inlets: A fresh-air inlet improves fireplace draft and usually forestalls back-puffing of smoke.

Fireplaces may draw a volume of air equal to two or three large roomfuls out through the chimney at frequent intervals. Thus, in tightly-constructed, efficiently weather-stripped houses, enough replacement of air cannot be drawn indoors to supply the chimney draft. A partial vacuum results, pulling smoke and combustion gases back into the room.

The fresh-air circulator draws outdoor air through a grille in the outside wall of the fireplace masonry or through a pipe connected with an outside wall opening located elsewhere.

LOCATION OF OUTLETS

You can place heated-air outlets anywhere it is convenient. The front or side faces of the fireplace masonry are the usual locations. They may be placed directly over the fireplace opening, in the mantel ledge above, or in the front or sides of the chimney wall close to the ceiling.

If you can't locate the outlet anywhere but the front wall above the fireplace opening, you can

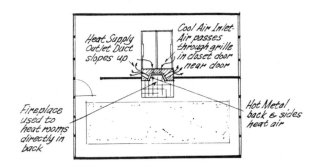

conceal it with a light shield of the same material as the walls.

A combination of outlets is practical. An outlet close to the ceiling on each side of the fireplace will distribute heated air to its part of the living room.

Warm air ducts placed just under the ceiling, inlets near floor, do not interrupt simple lines of fireplace facing

Air-circulating ducts are at the sides of brick fireplace in basement game room. Inner hearth is slightly recessed

OTHER FIREPLACE TYPES

Air-circulating units may be installed in conjunction with a metal hood, which hides a front outlet. Special

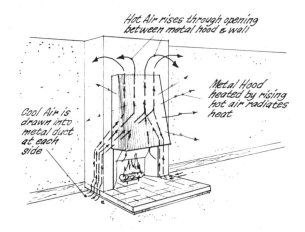

forms are built for see-through and projecting-corner fireplaces also.

HEATING OTHER ROOMS

The modified fireplace unit also can supply heated air to rooms behind the fireplace if ducts and outlets are provided.

Likewise heated air may be supplied to rooms back of or at the side of a corner fireplace. A standard recirculating unit with rear inlet openings designed for corner installation is available. You can also heat upper-floor rooms by recirculating heated air from the fireplace. Use a supplementary ventilating fan if you wish to be sure this unit will spread heat uniformly. Of course, any change from the manufacturer's standard position of inlets and outlets requires additional expense for fireproof piping.

***

Tracy Moberg, design; Charles Pearson, photo

Top: Air circulating unit built into shell of fieldstone masonry. Cold air intake through slots in base, warm air outlet through rock grating above lintel. Stonework matches walls

Center: Fireplace constructed of Roman and common brick. It has inlets and outlets formed of spaced brick. Metal frame holding firescreen is supported by the raised hearth

John C. Campbell and Worley Wong, design; Max Heinegg, photo

Bottom: Louvered grille runs width of top for warm air outlet, two grates in base squares draw in cold air. Natural finish combed wood frames large tiles. Wood storage left

Marvin S. Iles, design

Heat-circulating unit made for the projecting-corner fireplace has standard aluminum grilles for cool air inlets. One is in the pilaster at left. The other, at floor level under built-in settee, has an air duct leading into unit. All other inlets and outlets are of spaced masonry

Coffin and Mitchell, design; Sussman-Ochs, photo

Fireplace uses form specially designed for a see-through unit. Inlets and outlets on other side are spaced masonry

Francis Joseph McCarthy, design; Ernest Braun, photo

Outlets are slit into the facing, which is pre-finished industrial aluminum siding. Same material is used on the roof

Sink

Electric Burner

Fireplace Grill

Chinese Oven

Door to oven firebox

Vladimir Ossipoff, design; R. Wenkam, photo

Versatile outdoor combination can solve almost any cooking problem. Besides a fireplace with separate grill for broiling, it has a Chinese oven, electric spit attachment, built-in electric range, and a sink with cold running water

Barbecue and fireplace

The earliest fireplaces, those that graced the caves of our ancestors, were really barbecues. And today's home owner often feels the urge to cook over the open flames, anything from a marshallow to a whole roasted fowl.

If you plan to use your masonry and chimney for two fireplaces (see pages 52–54), you might make your second fireplace a barbecue. Or you can build a unit that will serve both as fireplace and barbecue. In fact, if you are careful, you can even barbecue with good results in an ordinary, well-built fireplace.

When a fireplace and barbecue are built as separate units, each needs a flue of its own, or the smoke from one is liable to pour down into the other. The flues should be separately capped or of different heights to avoid downdrafts.

FIREPLACE-BARBECUE COMBINATION

With a barbecue and fireplace combined in a single unit, you should have only one flue—but the flue should be at least one size larger than necessary for an ordinary fireplace with the same opening area. Grease smoke is

Morgan Stedman, design; Ernest Braun, photo

Fireplace in a wall of adobe. All metal is black wrought steel. Tile counter matches brick red patio tile on floor

SMOKE OVEN

INCINERATOR OUTSIDE

WARMING OVEN

WOODBOX (fills outside)

GRILL-ROTISSERIE

WOODBOX

FIREBOX

Art Hupy, photo

Barbecue wall in this family room addition has a grill and rotisserie combination in the raised fireplace, smoke oven (top) **connected by a flue with a firebox (lower right), and a warming oven which gets its heat by proximity to the flue**

heavier than wood smoke, and barbecuing tends to create sudden puffs that need to be carried off.

According to many experts, the flue should be still larger if you have a recessed firebed, because the low-ered firebox is shielded from the draft. It is wise to build a high smoke shelf, which will help to prevent grease smoke from rolling back down into the firebox. In some cases, a fan in the flue is desirable.

Some experts recommend a multi-controlled damper, one that opens and closes by degrees. Open it wide at the beginning of your barbecue session. After the initial heavy smoke is carried off, the barbecue should be al-most smokeless. Close down the damper to avoid losing heat.

If the fire has a proper draft, no grease should collect in the flue; but if grease does collect, you may anticipate flash fires in the chimney. A flue with a clay liner or a double liner will reduce fire hazard. Surrounding the flue with masonry will also help to prevent fire. Consult your fire marshal before building the barbecue-fireplace.

FIREPLACE AS BARBECUE

An ordinary fireplace with a multi-controlled damper and a generous, well-built flue can be used for barbe-cuing if you take care to prevent the mess that can re-sult from dripping, spattering grease. Protect the front hearth with a covering of aluminum foil or newspapers. Grease is almost impossible to remove from brick and tile.

See also the following *Sunset* books: *Ideas for Building Barbecues* and the *Barbecue Cook Book*.

The Dick McNeills, design; Frank L. Gaynor, photo

The fireplace-grill divides living and dining areas. It is tile-faced, has a raised hearth for "staging" dishes

Shish kebab attachment automatically turns each separate skewer a quarter turn during each cycle

Ernest Braun, photo

Steel supporting pole has extension screw that clamps inside the fireplace. A short sleeve with tightening screw mechanism holds grill, spit or motorized shish kebab assembly firmly in place

You can install a hand-cranked spit for meat cookery or an electric motor-driven spit, or sling a pot on a crane, or use a black iron Dutch oven right in the coals

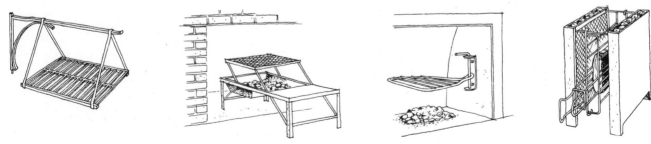

You can design your own grill, have it made in a metal shop. Here are four custom designs—two with their own charcoal containers for horizontal and vertical cooking

Brick fireplace and Dutch sideboard are opposite work areas in living-kitchen. A "cave" in the brick work holds wood for the fireplace. Pine settle table may be adjusted to form bench in front of fireplace. Pine paneling covers the kitchen walls

Dinner beside the hearth

Many years ago, the fireplace was the core of the kitchen. In its primitive way, it performed as range, oven, furnace, hot-water heater, garbage disposal unit, and clothes dryer. These functions are all performed today by an array of energetic appliances, but the fireplace still is on hand in many modern kitchens. And with good reason.

Architects have recognized that the typical American family likes to hang around the kitchen, and they have designed kitchen-dining rooms that are comfortable and inviting, a friendly place in which to visit, eat, play cards, do homework, or, incidentally, cook. To create an atmosphere of warmth and over-all good fellowship, designers have used warm-toned woods, amiable wallpapers, and, crowning asset, small, raised fireplaces.

Most fireplaces in kitchen-dining rooms are equipped with cooking facilities, such as a barbecue grill or a pot crane. Here the family chef can broil his sputtering fare without the help of time clocks.

For additional photographs, see the chapter on barbecue-fireplace combinations and the *Sunset* book, *Ideas for Building Barbecues.*

Paneling of hand-carved mahogany on the kitchen cupboards matches wood over the fireplace, which is of Roman brick

Norwood and DeLonge, design; Jerry Anson, photo

Fireplace of used brick with raised hearth is heart of this kitchen. Pine woodwork gives Early American look. Brick is continued behind cupboard

Esther Born, photo

Used brick fireplace graces one end of this dining-kitchen. Raised hearth and tile floor

Sumner Spaulding, design; Jerry Anson, photo

Corner of fireplace with brick and glass has spacious feeling. Brick fireplace wall continues outside. Hearth of dressed stone

James Lyon, design; Jerry Anson, photo

A fireplace and barbecue are combined in this dining end of a dining-kitchen. Chimney exterior painted white, red inside

William Aplin, photo

White-painted brick fireplace with curved lintel doubles as either fireplace or barbecue. Grill rests on projecting ledges when in use

Lutah Maria Riggs, design; Ernest Braun, photo

Fireplace with high raised hearth brings the fire to eye level. Black steel drawer is for charcoal

K. S. Brown, photo

Dressed stone hearth, fireplace opening blend with knotty pine wall in a casual kitchen-dining room

William Aplin, photo

Plastered adobe fireplace with raised hearth and red tile floor brightens dining corner. Glass-topped, steel table folds into cupboard for storage

Wurster, Bernardi, and Emmons, design; Ernest Braun, photo

Ernest Braun, photo

Kitchen-family room has modest brick fireplace that can be seen from the stove, dining table. View is of terrace

Dining room fireplace, used for either warmth or cooking. Ledges support barbecue grill, and double as serving shelf

Jerry Anson, photo

Jerry Anson, photo

Two fireplaces, oven, use this chimney. Oven at right of chimney. Fireplace warms dining room

Cooking can be done in fireplace or barbecue-oven at right in dining end of this comfortable kitchen. Polished wood mantel set in masonry

Jerry Anson, photo

An entire corner of this kitchen-dining room is bricked from ceiling to floor. Fireplace and barbecue unit share the wall

John V. Lesley, design; Ron Partridge, photo

Serviceable as well as attractive is this hooded fireplace in living-dining room. Raised tiled hearth accommodates utensils

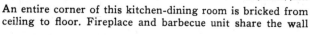

William Scott, design; Jerry Anson, photo

Knotty pine walls surround elevated white-painted adobe fireplace. Dining room, kitchen share view of this corner fireplace

Francis A. Constable, design; Ernest Braun, photo

Brick hearth of this two-faced fireplace continues around to living room opening. Used brick capped with patterned hood

William Aplin, photo

Combination barbecue and fireplace in airy outdoor room. Gas plate at left and sink at right, with built-in cupboards below.

Red brick unit forms corner of garden wall surrounding room. Tile counter tops on unit. Wood storage locker below gas plate

The outdoor-indoor room

A fireplace is a welcome asset in an outdoor-indoor room, such as a lanai, a roofed patio, or a deep porch.

Although outdoor-indoor rooms are protected from the weather, many of them need the added encouragement of a fireplace to shrug off a summer's fog or sunset chill. By taking the nip out of the night air, the hearth lengthens the evening's enjoyment; by carrying summer warmth well into autumn, it lengthens the season of enjoyment. In a lively room such as this, the crackling flames warm up the party.

Many fireplaces in outdoor-indoor rooms either contain provisions for barbecuing or are paired off with a separate barbecue unit. The room is a natural location for a barbecue. Informal meals can be prepared and downed on the spot, or the barbecue supper can be carried out into the garden or into the dining room indoors. The unit is close enough to the kitchen to take advantage of its stock of provisions, utensil supply, and standby cooking capacity.

Many fireplaces and barbecues share a common chimney. (Further samples may be found in the chapter on barbecue-fireplace combinations and in the *Sunset* book, *Ideas for Building Barbecues.*)

Maynard Parker, photo

Small fireplace is built into rough plastered wall in corner of this indoor-outdoor dining room. Tile steps for plants

Fireplace on lanai is made of broken-up concrete sidewalk. Patterned glass overhead cuts the glare. Terra cotta flue

Fireplace and barbecue unit, of Roman brick, make this pine paneled retreat combined cooking-dining-entertaining center

In a screened outdoor room, heavy steel of metal fireplace can take wind and rain. Used as a barbecue and for warmth

Heavy dressed stonework of fireplace continued in back wall under windows. Triangular flag shelves provided for plants

Hennig and Mushkin, design; Art Hupy, photo

Fireplace became the focal point for new family room, which grew from enclosed patio shown in the sketch. Roof was added first, to protect outdoor furniture from rain. Then the sides were enclosed, auxiliary heat added. The translucent glass on fireplace wall screens out the neighboring house. Note wood storage flanking fireplace

Ernest Braun, photo

Projecting-corner fireplace adds warmth to a roofed patio. Common brick laid jack-on-jack. Barbecue in background

E. J. Callahan, design; Tom Burns, Jr., photo

Enclosed swimming pools develop high humidity. This see-through fireplace helps ventilate as well as warm the pool

Edwards and Morrison, design; Charles Pearson, photo

H. H. Green, design; Stuart Weiner, photo

Roman brick wall of outdoor living room holds fireplace and elevating barbecue grill under hood. White tile mantel

Fireplace in this garden room is double. It serves both the patio and recreation room, located on the other side

Harold W. Hall, design; Charles Pearson, photo

Large fireplace makes wide circle of warmth on cool evenings. Roof of heat-absorbing glass cuts down wind, summer heat.

Barbecue left of fireplace, supplemented by refrigerator, sinks, counter built into wall. Masonry is dressed, fitted sandstone

Virgil Jorgenson, design; Philip Fein, photo

Outdoor fireplace of sandstone. Behind closed doors, between it and outdoor kitchen at right are wood storage, telephone.

Fireplace backed up to redwood exterior of house. Sheltered by overhang of cedar roof. Games stored at left of fireplace

Fireplaces under the sun

Outdoor fireplaces differ in several respects from their indoor relatives. Being located in free circulating air, they do not require the tall chimney that an indoor fireplace needs to draw air from an enclosed room. They can get by with short, stubby chimneys, or none at all. For the same reason, their inner workings can be planned with a somewhat freer hand than for indoor types. The damper is omitted, often the smoke shelf as well. The reflecting back and side walls of the firebox are usually not constructed so exactingly.

Most open-air fireplaces double as incinerators. They are thus built with generous fireboxes and large flues to carry off the smoke volume given off by burning trash.

Usually, an outdoor fireplace is found in company with a barbecue or else it has its own built-in provisions for grilling and roasting food. As the photographs indicate, the combination units are usually built alongside an outdoor dining area, where the reassuring warmth of the fire may be enjoyed by the diners at close range.

For further examples, see the *Sunset* book, *Ideas for Building Barbecues.*

Lester Lee Jones, design; Charles Pearson, photo

Outdoor fireplace is open on two sides, flames can be seen from inside dining room as well as terrace. Exhibit spot for kettles

William Aplin, photo

Top, left: Simple outdoor fireplace becomes barbecue when removable grill is placed in rack above embers. Hot plate on left was formerly an old stove top converted to barbecue use

William Aplin, photo

Top, right: Freestanding brick unit has fireplace, barbecue grill and oven located beyond porch. It serves as garden partition between two terraces. Brickwork softened by tree shade

Wurster, design; Roger Sturtevant, photo

Above: Fireplace attached to house forms center of interest in walled outdoor room. Fireplace built of concrete blocks, as is rest of house; brick lining to firebox, common brick hearth

Fred Oldendorf, design; Jerry Anson, photo

Center: Fireplace-barbecue walls-in entire play area. At right of fireplace is wood storage, at left is barbecue with grill

Ernest Braun, photo

Lower, right: Fireplace-barbecue in outdoor room has chimney to carry off smoke, hood to radiate heat. Cone of hood, half-filled with sand, keeps area warm long after fire dwindles

Jerry Anson, photo

Painted adobe fireplace, design from European peasant fireplace. Fluted chimney breast, of plaster, patted into shape by hand

Firelight in the bedroom

Bedrooms today are usually placed last on the list when fireplaces are being assigned on the house plans.

Yet this is an engaging luxury — as anyone can attest who has been lulled to sleep on a frosty night by the flicker of a dying fire in a bedroom hearth.

A fireplace also converts a bedroom to daytime use as a sitting room, cozy for sewing, reading, conversing. Some of the bedrooms pictured here have many of the qualities of a second living room.

Note that most of the fireplaces pictured are elevated types, raised above floor level so the fire may be seen and enjoyed from the bed.

A bedside fireplace offers no greater fire hazard than one in any other room, provided it is equipped with a trustworthy firescreen that will contain all flying sparks and embers.

Austin Pierpont, design; William Aplin, photo

Living end of this bedroom is graced by corner fireplace of half bricks, view of garden terrace. Note three-sided hearth

Wendell Lovett, design; Darrow M. Watt, photo
Guest house near family cabin has a prefabricated metal fireplace which relieves plainness of simply furnished bedroom-sitting room combination

Maynard Parker, photo
Fireplace, elevated with semi-circular hearth, forms part of alcove which holds table, seats

Tad Nichols, photo
Corner fireplace in this bedroom is white plaster and is topped by triangular chimney

George Bristol, design; Morley Baer, photo
Hood in this bedroom fireplace is painted black. It is backed by wall of brick and shares chimney with the living room fireplace. Redwood bed built-in

Chapin Bowen, photo

Stone fireplace and log rafters, beams, and railings combine to give air of rugged rusticity to cabin. Log-railed balcony, crossing fireplace chimney breast, connects hobby rooms on both sides. Mantel in this cabin is formed of three long stones

Cabin fireplaces

Fireplaces built in cabins—whether in the mountains, in the desert, or along the seacoast—are expected to perform valiantly during the short season that they are in use.

As most of them provide the sole source of heat in a cabin, they are often installed with hot-air circulating units. Without such a booster, many of them would be unable to hold their own against the chilly mountain night or the damp onshore breezes.

Cabin fireplaces have some structural peculiarities. When they are built of rock quarried on the landsite, they must be constructed of fire-resistant stone or else they disintegrate. If situated at altitudes above 2,000 feet, they require higher chimneys or larger flues than at sea level because of the thinner air. As they are often subjected to wide extremes of temperature—hot, dry summers, frosty falls, and freezing winters—they require frequent inspection for frost damage and cautious firing in spring to thaw the waterlogged masonry. Their chimneys require a tight-fitting metal cap to prevent birds from nesting in the flue, and rodents from entering the cabin.

Howard B. Hoffman, photo

Massive stone fireplace built around heat circulating unit. Heavy mantel helps support roof trusses; firetenders are warned of low mantel by a series of cones hung before fire

Ulysses Floyd Rible, design; Woodcock, photo

Rugged fireplace of heavy stones forms one wall in this room. Raised hearth creates room for wood storage space

Charles Pearson, photo

Brick masonry is set in steps, used as stairway to sleeping quarters. Fire screen slips across opening on rod

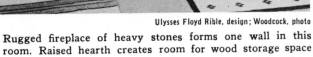

Alan McRae, design; Art Hupy, photo

Left: Copper fireplace hangs from the masonry chimney and generates enough heat to warm the entire cabin most months

William F. Hempel, design; Roger Sturtevant, photo

Lower left: Monterey stone fireplace forms corner wall in woodland cabin. Visible from kitchen, living, dining room

Bob and Ira Spring, photo

Lower right: Brick facing is fitted into a cabin built of cedar logs. Log veneer over chimney breast. Logs form furniture

P. A. Dearborn, photo

Warm knotty cedar paneling of fireplace and walls extends to ceiling, creating a feeling of space in this cabin living room

Francis Palms, Jr., design; Darrow M. Watt, photo

Small but functional cabin fireplace is used for heat and some cooking. Sheet metal hood and raised concrete hearth

Bob Jones, design; Morley Baer, photo

Adobe brick fireplace blends with natural waxed knotty pine paneling. Flush tile hearth provides contrast to the fireplace

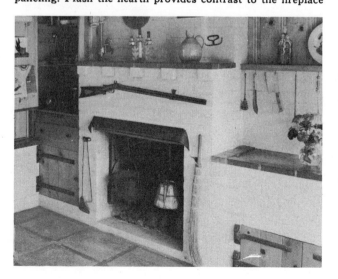

Bernice Blundon, photo

Above: Large stones face fireplace which is backed on knotty pine walls. Four heat circulating ducts at front. Beam mantel

Max Tatch, photo

Cabin fireplace doubles as cooking unit; equipped with two pot cranes. Tile topped, painted; brick facing contrasts with panels

George T. Rockrise, design; Tom Burns, Jr., photo

Above: Heat-circulating fireplace has vents at the side. The facing is native stone gathered near the cabin site

Wendell Lovett, design; John Bickel, photo

Above, right: Prefabricated metal fireplace has a gravel "beach," contained by aluminum garden edging, for a hearth

George Kosmak, design; Ernest Braun, photo

Right: Fireplace is volcanic stone with firebrick at back and sides. Wrought iron hood is finished with stove black

Robert H. Hartman, design; Ernest Braun, photo

Below, left: Walls of three-cornered living room converge on fireplace at far end. Raised tile hearth is also seat

Below, right: Stone fireplace in log cabin has circulating heat installation that sends warm air to all corners of room

Fireplace facelifting

If the appearance of your present fireplace distresses you, there are several simple things that you can do about it.

A worn, tired-looking face can be freshened up easily and inexpensively with a coat of paint. Select the same color as the walls or one that harmonizes or contrasts. Or it may be concealed behind a false front. As shown in the photographs, a new facing of corrugated iron or cast concrete panels may be set right over the old one. Another good idea is to swallow it up in a set of bookshelves. The example on a following page shows how simple shelving can be used to tie an isolated and uninteresting fireplace into a room and improve the room at the same time.

If you like to do things the hard way, you can chip off the facing and build a new one. As usually happens in such a case, the replacement of the facing leads to replacement of other elements, such as cupboards, bookcases, etc. A dispirited fireplace is often teamed with an impossible room, its main wall cut up with small windows or misplaced doors. Remodeling, therefore, calls for doing the whole room over.

For a really tough assignment, you can try tearing out the firebox and rebuilding the whole works. This is sometimes unavoidable if an old damper unit is to be replaced or a heat circulating unit added. But it is a mean, hazardous, and dirty job that should be reserved for a master mason—if he'll take it on.

One clever way to remodel is to turn the fireplace around so it faces into the room in back. This is done by knocking out the back wall, covering over the front, and building a new facing in the back room. Like this:

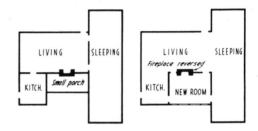

Again, this, too, is a job for a skillful brickmason.

Stone and Steccati, photo

Old kitchen chimney converted into 9-foot-high fireplace with 20 by 30-inch opening. Corrugated asbestos cement panels bolted to wooden frame, fitted over old facing. Bolts roughed with sandpaper. Shelves added to fill waste space at either side

A. S. Dudley, photo

Large fireplace fills opening once occupied by garage doors. The hearth, 14 inches above the floor, constructed of stone. Timber recessed in wall forms mantel. Crane has four hooks for cooking. Fireplace in recreation room made from garage

Herman V. Wall, photo

Above: Before alteration, dining room wall cut by ugly fireplace and closet door. *Right:* Fireplace given marble facing and hearth and ornate firescreen. Wall paneled in redwood, painted. Mirror was added to give depth. Frame removed from closet door, painted, blends into the wall

John L. Field, design; Morley Baer, photo

Remodeling the eyesore you see sketched above was relatively simple. The mantel was replaced by a sheet metal hood built out the same depth as the existing fireplace. Facing is terra cotta tile

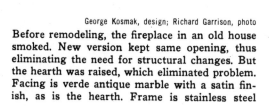

George Kosmak, design; Richard Garrison, photo

Before remodeling, the fireplace in an old house smoked. New version kept same opening, thus eliminating the need for structural changes. But the hearth was raised, which eliminated problem. Facing is verde antique marble with a satin finish, as is the hearth. Frame is stainless steel

Paul Kirk, design; Dearborn-Massar, photo

New ceramic tile set over the existing brick simplified the fireplace design. Another fireplace is below, in basement

William Aplin, photo

When family room was added, bricks were cut from the back wall of a conventional fireplace, making it a see-through

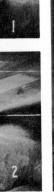

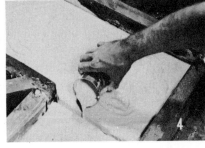

Sculptured cement fireplace, cast by hand, completely changes aspects of this room. Facing made in three steps: a clay mold, plaster cast, and the finished product. (1) Design cut into clay mold with wire hollowing tool; (2) gouge marks smoothed with soft brush dipped in water; (3) plaster poured over clay to form mold; (4) additional plaster poured around joints so three molds will form continuous cast. Cement is then poured, producing (5) the finished panel ready to install

Above: Cheerless line-up of bookcases and fireplace in living room made ceiling seem low. Windows break up wall space. *Left:* Room comes to life with fireplace rebuilt with raised hearth and used brick facing. Bookshelves extended to ceiling add height to room. Windows become part of unit

Fuels and first aid

If a fireplace is to perform at peak efficiency it should be supplied with the best available fuels, provided with practical and appropriate tools and accessories, and examined periodically for infirmities.

WOOD TO BURN

Every firetender has his own favorite woods. Usually, choice is limited to the kinds that grow nearby, since it is economically impractical to haul firewood long distances. Where any choice is permitted, hardwood is preferred over soft for a long-burning fire, and softwood is favored for a rip-snorting, crackling blaze. The hardwoods are considered to include: oak, hickory, madrone, manzanita, maple, and eucalyptus. Popular softwoods include pine, poplar, fir, and elm.

The heat given off by hard or soft wood is about equal, but hardwood, being denser, burns longer, forms longer-lasting coals, and leaves less residue.

Size of the logs is figured from the standard 4-foot cord measure. Most popular fireplace length is half-cord size, or 24 inches. Smaller size, known as stove length, is cut to 16 inches; and a 3-foot log is also available for large-size fireplaces.

Variations: Some firetenders prefer charcoal or a mixture of charcoal and wood. Charcoal gives off an impressive amount of heat—twice that of wood, pound for pound. It heats by direct radiation, and, once started, it burns long and steadily. Charcoal briquets often give off more heat than the raw form and they burn without sparking. Charcoal is favored for barbecuing in the fireplace. *Caution:* Because of the danger of being overcome by carbon monoxide (which can not be detected by the senses), always provide ample ventilation when burning charcoal in an enclosed area.

Logs of compressed sawdust offer an effective, if relatively expensive, fuel. They burn with greater heat than wood, giving off 75 per cent of the heat of coal.

Aroma and Color: A wide variety of woods burn with pleasing aroma and color. Dried chunks of pine blaze with enthusiasm and a woodsy odor. Eucalyptus is pungent; even a handful of pods from the tree produces a fragrant odor.

For colorful flame, no fuel can match driftwood for its blue and lavender fire. Aged pieces of apple-wood also burn with rainbow colors and an appealing fragrance.

Colorful fire may also be produced by chemical means. Copper chloride produces strong blue and green flames, but will also yield some purple, pink, and yellow fire. Copper chloride in technical crystals is preferable to the chemically pure form. If mixed with other chemicals, it should be blended in a glass container, as it deposits copper plating on any metal that it touches.

For a strong red flame, use strontium chloride, or if it is not obtainable, strontium nitrate. It may be mixed with copper chloride to add to the rainbow effect.

Common table salt (sodium chloride) gives off a brilliant yellow fire. It tends to cancel out other colors, so use it sparingly in combinations. If you wish to mix these three chemicals, blend 2 parts copper chloride with 1 part each of strontium chloride and table salt.

Chemicals may be tossed directly on the fire, or they may be mixed with water and soaked into the fuel ahead of time. Pine cones and charcoal should be immersed in the solution for several hours.

SMOKING

The commonest complaint about a malfunctioning fireplace usually centers on smoking. This annoying habit may be caused by a number of factors, but fortunately, it is usually curable. Here are the main causes and cures:

1. Fireplace opening is too large for the flue. *Cure:* Since enlargement of the flue is practically impossible, a reduction in size of the fireplace opening is the answer. This can be done by raising the hearth, bringing in the sides, or lowering the top with masonry or a hood.

2. Damper may be set in place too low. *Cure:* Lower the top of the fireplace opening. Damper may be moved up, but this is a major operation. You can also get a specially designed damper that is lowered easily 6 inches into the top of the flue. It has a long, alloy chain that drops into the firebox.

3. Efficient weatherstripping will not admit enough air into the house to feed the fire. *Cure:* Open a window 2 or 3 inches.

4. Hot air furnace draws air away from the fireplace. *Cure:* Open a window.

5. Side-by-side flues with uncemented joints between the linings permit leakage between flues, causing down-drafts and smoke leaks. *Cure:* Fill all cracks with mortar.

6. Chimney is too short to provide proper draft. *Cure:* Add metal or terra cotta extension on cap.

7. Nearby trees or buildings or a steep roof line cause wind to blow down chimney. *Cure:* Extend flue lining with cement bevel or tile cap, or divert wind currents away from chimney opening with baffles or a patent cap.

8. Structural defects, such as off-center flues, sharp angle in flue passage, projection of pipes into flues, double use of single flue, etc. *Cure:* Call for professional help.

LEAKING

Water seepage around a chimney or fireplace is an obstinate ailment to trace down and eliminate, because water follows a circuitous course from its point of original entry. First place to look is the flashing around the fireplace and at the roof line. Check the mastic seal, look for nails that have not been sealed over, check for ruptured seams and joints caused by settling of house or masonry. Often, frost action will crack mortar and admit water through the brickwork itself. Check and repair all joints. If chimney cap is not beveled to shed rain water, add a sloped cap of smoothed mortar.

CLEANING FIREPLACE FACING

When the face of your fireplace becomes stained with smoke and soot, it may be cleaned with a mild acid bleach, such as vinegar or commercial acetic acid, or with a scouring of strong soap and water. If the stain does not yield to this treatment, it may require stronger measures. A solution of muriatic acid will often do the job, although it should never be used on stonework and it may discolor brickwork. Mix 10 parts water in 1 part acid in a wide-mouthed glass jar and apply with a rag. Rinse off with water immediately. Raw muriatic acid (a parlor name for hydro-chloric acid) is a powerful chemical and should be handled with respect.

One good way to make the clean-up task easier is not to get the fireplace dirty. To prevent blackening the facing, avoid burning trash in large amounts. Most fireplace flue proportions are not figured to accommodate the heavy blaze that a big load of paper will produce. Feed the paper slowly, in moderate amounts, and you won't have to worry about a discolored facing.

CHIMNEY CARE

Inspection: To inspect a chimney, lower a light on a weighted extension cord. Look for loose or fallen bricks, cracks or breaks in the flue lining. Check on the degree of sooting. Inspect outside of chimney by prodding mortar joints with a knife to test for loose mortar.

Cleaning: If the fireplace is used continuously, a thorough chimney cleansing is an annual must. A weighted sack stuffed with hay, or a scratchy bush, may be pulled up and down the flue to dislodge the accumulation of soot. *Important:* The front of the fireplace should be sealed off while the chimney is being cleaned, otherwise soot will flow into the room. By far the cleanest method is to have the flue vacuumed by professional chimney cleaners.

Some chemical compounds are available for burning out the soot. Fire authorities recommend crystalline compounds as being best for this operation. If the soot accumulation is unusually heavy, however, it is probably more safely removed by mechanical means.

Repairing: To fill joints and cracks inside the chimney lining, lower a weighted bag down the chimney. It should fit just loosely enough to slide up and down. Park the bag alongside the crack to be filled, pour a stream of grout onto the top of the bag, and work it into the open seam. Slide bag up and down to remove excess filler, and move along to the next crack. Loose mortar on the outside should be pried out, the open joint dampened, and new mortar forced in.

Chimney Fires: Although most chimneys will probably withstand the heat of a chimney fire, flames may pass through a crack into the walls, or burning flakes of soot may ignite the roof. If your chimney breaks into flame, first step is to call the fire department. While you wait for the firemen, or if your fireplace is beyond fire service, you can help by throwing salt or baking soda on the fire in the grate and dousing the roof with the garden hose.

How to build it right

Fireplace construction is hemmed in by a host of rules, formulas, and craft practices. Here are the basic requirements.

FOUNDATION

The foundation that supports both fireplace and chimney should extend into the soil at least 12 inches. In cold climate regions, the bottom of the foundation should be below frost line.

Reinforced concrete or solid masonry foundations will sustain weight of chimney and fireplace without sagging. The concrete slab should be strengthened with a grid of ½-inch reinforcing bars, placed 12 inches apart, and set at least 3 inches above the bottom of the slab. Foundations should be 6 to 12 inches wider all around than the chimney. Fireplace and chimney should never be supported by wooden floors, beams, or posts, because in time they will shrink or bend under the load and fracture the masonry.

MORTAR

Use cement mortar for the entire chimney and flue construction. Recommended proportions are: 1 part Portland cement, 4½ parts mortar sand, ½ part fireclay. Add enough water to produce a fairly stiff mix. This mix may also be used in the firebox, preferably with slightly thinner joints.

ASH PIT

The ash dump and pit are conveniences to consider if construction permits their installation. They should be protected, however, from water, for if the ash load becomes water-soaked, it will permeate the house with a disagreeable ashy odor.

Cover the opening to the dump with a cast iron plate (about 5x8 inches), pivoted or hinged to allow ashes to drop into the pit below. Select a type that will not drop accidentally into the pit when opened. The dump cover is usually placed near the center of the back hearth, but it can be located anywhere in the back hearth if desired.

To promote easy ash removal, raise the sill of the clean-out door approximately 10 inches above grade or the basement floor for placement of ash receptacle, and cover the bottom with mortar sloped toward the door.

For a fireplace on a second floor, directly above the living room hearth, it is necessary to route the ash chute around the fireplace below. The change of direction should not be greater than 60 degrees to avoid ash retardation. Many second story fireplaces are built without an ash dump.

FACING

For safety, the nearest edge of wood trim, paneling, or surfacing should be at least 8 inches from the sides of the fireplace opening and at least 12 inches above the top of the opening. Maintain a minimum clearance of 2 inches between all wood framing members and the fireplace or chimney masonry. Make the front hearth at least 8 to 12 inches wider on each side than the fireplace opening.

FIREPLACE DIMENSIONS

To assure proper heating and to prevent smoking, follow closely fireplace dimensions given in the chart. Too much variation will cause a fireplace to smoke and diminish the amount of heat it supplies.

Fireplace Dimensions (In inches)	
Width	24 to 84
Height	2/3 to 3/4 width
Depth	1/2 to 2/3 height
Flue Effective Area	1/8 width x height—Unlined flue 1/10 width x height—Rectang. lining 1/12 width x height—Round lining
Throat Area	1/4 to 1/2 larger than flue area
Throat Width	3" minimum to 4½" maximum

FIREBOX

Back hearth and reflecting walls should be of soapstone or firebrick, 4 inches thick, or hard-burned tile, 3 inches thick. This thickness includes the fireclay mortar holding hearth or wall in place.

To lessen the danger of bricks loosening or falling out, lay firebricks flat. On edge, they are only 2 inches thick and should be held in place by metal ties bonded into the main masonry walls.

If you build the back wall in the shape of a vertical curve sloping into the fireplace, not only rising currents of warm air but smoke will flow into the room. To avoid a smoky fireplace, slope the profile of the back wall up in straight planes above the level of the lintel to the edge of the throat.

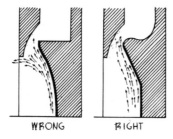

WRONG RIGHT

LINTEL

The minimum lintel required to support the masonry above the front of a moderately wide fireplace opening is an angle iron 3½ by 3½ by ¼ inches, and enough longer than the opening to give a 3- or 4-inch seat on the masonry. For heavy masonry and wide openings, the size and thickness of these iron lintels increase in proportions.

You can build a masonry arch successfully if, at the sides of the opening, the masonry is sufficiently strong to resist the thrust of the arch. The minimum thickness of masonry in front of the lintel or forming the masonry arch should be 4 to 6 inches, preferably more to avoid possible sagging.

DAMPER

There are many forms of dampers, usually combined with a metal throat. Some operate by means of a push-and-pull handle, some with a poker, others with a twist handle. You can be sure of good results

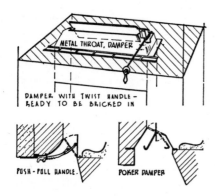

METAL THROAT, DAMPER

DAMPER WITH TWIST HANDLE — READY TO BE BRICKED IN

PUSH-PULL HANDLE.   POKER DAMPER

with any type that is installed according to manufacturers' directions. Dampers should be set loosely in place—the blade should rattle in a good wind—to allow for expansion.

THROAT

The throat, or damper opening, should extend the full width of the fireplace opening and have an area not less than that of the flue. Up to the throat, the sides of the fireplace should be vertical; about 5 inches above the throat, the sides should start drawing in to the flue. The bottom edge of the throat should be 6 to 8 inches or more above the bottom of the lintel. The throat can be formed in masonry. Better still, for a saving of time and labor, you can install a metal prefabricated throat.

SMOKE SHELF

The smoke shelf should run the full length of the throat and be 6 to 12 inches or more front to back, depending on the depth of the fireplace. It should be given a smooth, concave surface.

SMOKE CHAMBER

The smoke chamber extends between the side walls from the top of the throat to the bottom of the flue. Slope the side walls at an angle of 60 degrees from the horizontal, and smoothly plaster with cement mortar or an equally smooth interior surface so as not to diminish the draft action.

FLUES

Round flues are considered most efficient for draft and smoke removal because draft-smoke column ascends in round spirals. Corners of square or rectangular flues are ineffective areas, contributing little to proper working of a flue. Square or oblong flues are frequently used, however, because they are easier to set in place.

All authorities recommend that flues be lined with a smooth fireclay tile at least ⅝-inch thick. There are several advantages in using it. Lining reduces friction between draft column and masonry and lessens the amount of inflammable soot and creosote that clings to inside of flue. Lining also helps prevent cracking of masonry and mortar joints as chimney expands or contracts during alternate heating and cooling. Without lining, the mortar and brick exposed to hot flue gases will gradually disintegrate.

Don't accept a mortar substitute for the lining. Chimney movement due to wind and temperature changes may cause mortar to crack and fall. This results in partial stoppage with consequent loss of draft and increased fire hazard.

Flues have better draft if built as close to a vertical line as possible. When a change in direction is necessary, it should not exceed 30° from vertical nor should it reduce the flue area at the offset.

Multiple Flues: Each fireplace requires a separate flue, but you can locate two or more flues in one chimney. Separate them with a 4-inch brick or concrete divider wall, known as a "wythe."

Size: The capacity of the flue must match that of the fireplace. Following are recommended flue sizes for sea-level installation (see paragraph "Height of Chimney" for information on effect of altitude).

Recommended Flue Sizes (In inches)					
Fireplace Width	Rectangular Flues			Equivalent Round	
	Outside Dimension	Inside Dimension	Effective Area Sq. In.	Inside Diameter	Effective Area Sq. In.
24	8½x 8½	7¼x 7¼	41	8	50.3
30 to 34	8½x13	7 x11½	70	10	78.5
36 to 44	13 x13	11¼x11¼	99	12	113.0
46 to 56	13 x18	11¼x16¼	156	15	176.7
58 to 68	18 x18	15¾x15¾	195	18	254.4
70 to 84	20 x24	17 x21	278	22	380.13
Over 84	SIZES PROPORTIONATELY LARGER				

CHIMNEY MATERIALS

Many kinds of masonry, brick, concrete, concrete blocks, stone, or hollow clay tile, are suitable for chimney walls. Following are recommended minimum thicknesses for wall sections:

Brick: lined, not less than thickness of standard brick, 3¾ inches; exterior walls exposed to very severe weather not less than 8 inches. Unlined, not less than 8 inches with inner course preferably of firebrick.

Hollow tile or concrete blocks: lined, and not less than 8 inches.

Stone: lined, and not less than 12 inches.

Concrete: lined, not less than 4 inches. Unlined, not less than 6 inches. Concrete chimneys require vertical and horizontal lacing of steel reinforcing rod.

THE PATENT CHIMNEY

Patent or prefabricated chimneys sometimes substitute for masonry, and both are somewhat less expensive.

Patent chimneys consist of round metal flues lined with terra cotta and protected on the outside by metal casings. Building codes require at least 1 inch of clearance between outer casing and woodwork.

Prefabricated chimneys come in sections made up of two metal cylinders separated by insulating material. For further details and sketches, see the chapter on metal fireplaces.

INSULATION

Leave a fire stop space of 2 inches between all wood beams, joists, floors, and outside face of chimney walls. Fill this space with loose crushed cinders, mortar refuse, gypsum block, or other incombustible material. Solid mortar, concrete, or masonry is unsuited for this purpose.

If the chimney is at least 8 inches thick and lined, clearance between chimney and wood construction may be reduced to ½ inch. Authorities recommend adding a cement plaster coat to masonry chimneys that are to be encased by wood paneling or other combustible materials.

Set wall studs to insure 2-inch clearance between studs and chimney masonry. Plastering may be done directly on chimney wall or on raised metal lath laid over the masonry. Plaster directly on the wall is preferable because it will not crack when the chimney settles.

If exposed upper section of chimney is subject to severe winds, its walls should be at least 8 inches thick. If chimney walls are less, enlarge them, starting at least 8 inches from roof rafters or joist.

HEIGHT OF CHIMNEY

To prevent upward draft from being neutralized by downward eddies from neighboring roofs, build chimney flue at least 3 feet above flat roofs and 2 feet above ridge of pitched roofs. At elevations above 2,000 feet, height of chimney should be raised slightly or the flue area should be increased. Rough rule of thumb is to increase both height and cross-sectional area of the flue about 5 per cent for each 1,000 feet above sea level. Consult architects, local building inspectors, masonry contractors for data.

Where roof conditions keep you from going the recommended height above the roof, a tile chimney pot may give the effect of the necessary additional height. Chimney hoods of metal, brick, stone, or tile also prevent back drafts. Place hood with closed sides against direction of air currents. The open area of the hood should be at least 4 times the cross sectional area of the flue.

SPARK SCREENS

Spark arresting screens are an advisable safety measure if chimney is in a wooded area or close to dry vegetation. Use rust-resistant wire mesh or perforated sheet metal with openings not smaller than ½ nor larger than ⅝ inch. Top of screen should be at least 12 inches above cap.

Putting a fireplace together

Whether you build a fireplace yourself or just get in a mason's way while he builds one for you, you may find it helpful to know how one is assembled. At least you can understand what the craftsman is doing and what he is talking about.

As a matter of fact, there are probably as many ways of building a fireplace and chimney as there are brickmasons. Many masons feel that fireplace build-ins is an art, and no book of rules and equations will ever show *them* how to do their work.

The drawings that follow simply show in a general way the steps usually followed in building a simple fireplace. They are not assembly instructions, nor do they attempt to blanket all the variations that local building practices and ordinances bring about.

The building principles shown will apply roughly to almost any type of fireplace. Some variables: If the illustrated fireplace were built directly on a slab floor, it would still require a minimum of 12 inches of foundation slab, for the standard floor slab is not strong enough to hold the concentrated load. In some situations, the one-brick-wide walls would not be adequate. For instance, if the installation included a deep basement ash dump, or a second fireplace on a floor above, or a chimney taller than 8 feet above the plate. In some localities, two-brick-wide walls may be required throughout. Some local jurisdictions require that steel reinforcing rods be carried continuously from the foundation, through the firebox and throat, to the top of the chimney.

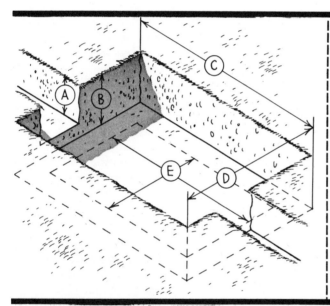

1. EXCAVATION

The size of the pit that is dug for the foundation slab is influenced by several factors. *Depth* (Dimension B) should never be less than 12 inches for a one-story chimney. Greater depth will be required if soil conditions are unstable, frost action is likely to be severe, and if the fireplace-chimney structure will have fireplaces on two floors. Note that the pit should run slightly below the bottom of the house foundation (Dimension A). *Outside dimensions* (C and D) should be at least 6 inches larger all around than the outer measurements of the chimney (Dimension E). Relation of Dimension D to position of the house foundation depends on how far into the room the fireplace facing will come.

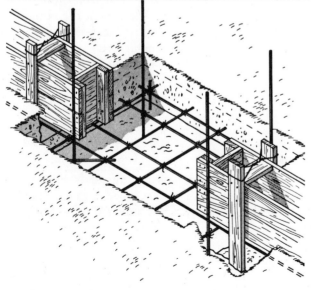

2. FORMS AND REINFORCING

The fireplace slab and the house foundation are usually poured at the same time. As top of the house foundation is higher than top of the fireplace slab, foundation forms are built to dam the concrete on each side of the slab. House foundation may be built to overlap the slab (as in drawing) so it will butt against the brick chimney base; or it may be stopped at the edge of the slab and the gap filled in later with brick. Note that top of slab should come just below grade. Reinforcing steel in house foundation is run right through slab. The slab is reinforced with a grid of ½-inch rods, 12 inches on center, supported 5 inches above bottom of pit by rods driven into the ground. Vertical corner rods sometimes required.

3. ASH PIT

Brickwork for the ash pit is laid directly on the slab. Care must be taken to make certain that the slab surface is absolutely clean of dirt, otherwise the bricks will not bond to the concrete. Some localities require 8-inch walls throughout. The two inner walls shown are optional. They are placed where they will support the brick firebox. Often, the floor of the ash pit is filled in with grout or masonry up to the level of the clean-out opening, to facilitate ash removal. If vertical steel reinforcements are required by local code, the bars should be sealed into the masonry as shown in the small detail.

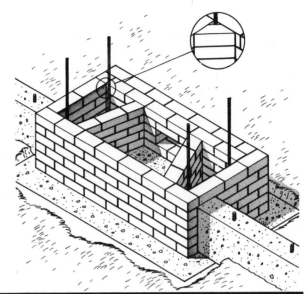

4. SUBHEARTH FORMS

This is one way of preparing for a reinforced concrete subhearth. Wet concrete is supported over rear hearth by a loose layer of bricks, resting on ½-inch steel rods set over ash pit. One brick is left out and a wooden box substituted to provide opening for ash drop. Front hearth is supported on wooden forms, removed after concrete has set. A grid of ½-inch reinforcing steel is laid 1 inch below top of slab. Alternate ways of building: (a) top of ash pit may be closed with wooden forms that are removed through the clean-out door after concrete has set; (b) front and back hearth may be supported on steel plates, specially made for the purpose; or (c) the whole subhearth may be made of brick.

5. FINISHED SUBHEARTH

This cut-away drawing shows the finished concrete slab in place. The slab, which is cantilevered out from the front wall of the ash pit, will be anchored under weight of brickwork to be laid on rear hearth. Any irregularities in surface—such as a low point above the brick roof—may be corrected with mortar when the finished hearth is laid. Note placement of reinforcing steel mat. Wooden forms that supported front hearth removed after concrete has set. *Note that the hearth is not attached in any way to the floor joists of house.* Vertical steel reinforcing rods are continued through slab to be cemented in brickwork around firebox.

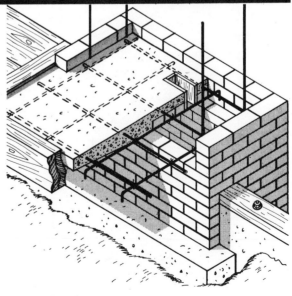

6. FINISHED HEARTH

The finished hearth may be laid as soon as the hearth slab has set and the outer brickwork has been brought up a few courses. The inner hearth is laid with firebrick, bonded to the subhearth with fireclay-cement mortar. Note that the firebrick floor covers only the area needed for the firebox. When these bricks have been laid, they are usually covered with a layer of sand to protect them from globs of mortar that may be dropped as the masonry grows. The front hearth—usually laid with tile or common brick—can be set at this time or postponed until the facing is laid in place. Note masonry ties, inserted in the mortar joints, for anchoring the facing when it is attached later.

FILL WITH BRICK SCRAP

24"-84"

20"-24"

30"-90"

20" min.

12" min.

7. FIREBOX

The firebrick walls of the firebox may be laid at the same time as the outer brickwork or they may be held off until the outer work reaches damper height. Firebricks are usually laid in a cement-fireclay mortar, mixed to consistency of soft butter, and applied in thin layer ⅛ to ¼ inch thick. Bricks are set on edge or laid flat. If laid flat, they give greater strength to the wall. Side walls are slanted inwards about 4 to 6 inches. The space between the side walls and the outer brickwork is either filled in with bricks or left open. Advantage of the brick fill: adds strength to firebox wall, keeps it from being damaged by a carelessly thrown chunk of firewood.

8. REFLECTING BACK WALL

The back wall is laid plumb for about 12 inches, then it is sloped forward to reflect heat outward and to provide for a smoke shelf. Angle of slant depends on size and height of fireplace. Side walls are usually laid to butt against it; hence, they have to be cut at back end to meet angle of the sloping wall. One way to cut side walls is to put top courses of brick in place dry, hold a straight board against the rear edge of the wall slanted at proper angle, and draw line along edge. Then, disassemble the upper wall, cut bricks on line, and mortar in place. After both side walls are laid, back wall may be buttered in. First course above straight wall is tipped by making a wedge-shaped joint, higher in back than in front.

9. DAMPER AND SMOKE SHELF

The damper is rested in place on top of the fire-box walls, in line with the smoke shelf. There are innumerable varieties of dampers, but they all belong in two main categories: blade and dome dampers. In the blade type, the damper door is hinged or swiveled in a flat frame. In the dome type (see drawing), the door is fitted into a metal housing shaped into a throat. Some dome dampers are designed with a front edge that serves as lintel for fireplace facing, but most of them simply support masonry of the inner brickwork. Dampers come with a choice of controls for opening and closing. Some controls extend through the facing, some work by chain, some (see drawing) are operated with a poker.

DOME DAMPER

10. PREFABRICATED FIREPLACE

An alternate method of building the firebox is to use a prefabricated metal shell that incorporates all the vital parts—firebox, damper, throat, smoke chamber, lintel, and flue collar. Installation of such a unit simplifies the task of building a fireplace, for the masonry is merely laid around it; and it insures proper and exact proportions of the critical parts. Metal units are manufactured in a choice of sizes and styles (the one in the drawing is a composite) by several firms. Most are equipped with hot-air circulating ducts that permit the fireplace to double as a hot-air furnace. (See chapter "The Fireplace as Furnace.") They are usually built in, with a surrounding mat of fiberglas to allow for expansion.

11. THROAT

The throat—point where the fireplace narrows down to chimney width—is a tricky part to construct. It requires careful cutting and fitting and on-the-spot adjusting of dimensions. First, straight courses are laid around the damper installation to give the blade room to open without hindrance. Then the sides and front are stepped inward. The one-brick-wide side walls change to two bricks in width for the six or seven courses required for them to narrow down to chimney width. Back wall remains straight. At the point where the chimney starts, a slight ledge is provided in the brickwork to support the flue tile. Note that house framing in front of the throat is placed 2 inches above the brickwork base below it.

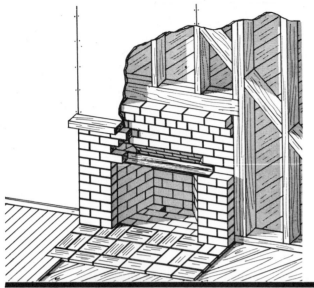

12. FACING

The finished facing may be applied at any time after the firebox is completed. Many masons prefer to complete the rough brickwork up to the chimney flue before installing the facing, others build the facing at the same time as the firebox. The facing is usually fashioned of either stone or brick, carefully leveled and struck with smooth mortar joints. It may be built to project into the room or it may be set flush with the wall, or even recessed slightly and paneled over. An iron lintel is placed two or three courses below the top of the firebox. It is rested loosely in the mortar joint on both sides, but the bricks are not mortared to it across the opening. If the front hearth is still to be laid, it may be finished at this time.

13. WEATHERSEAL AND CHIMNEY FLUE

At the point where the fireplace structure passes through the house walls, careful weathersealing is needed to prevent water from seeping in around the opening during the rainy season. This seal is usually effected by flashing with wide strips of metal, usually copper, bent to fit over the gaps and sealed in place with a caulking compound. Often, the brickwork is built with a jog so it locks into the opening. The chimney is usually lined with sections of terra cotta flue tile and strengthened with vertical steel rods, set in each corner. The tiles are set in place first and the masonry laid up around them. Where the chimney brickwork rests against the house sheathing, the woodwork is covered with weatherproof paper.

14. CHIMNEY TIE

In most localities, building codes require that the fireplace chimney be tied into the house structure at the roof line. This reinforcement tends to steady the chimney and keep it from parting from the house during an earthquake or a heavy windstorm or if either the house or fireplace structure settles a bit. There are many ways of tying the chimney into the structure. The drawing shows one method. A strap of 1-inch iron is bent around the flue tile and reinforcing steel, twisted to pass flat through a mortar joint, and the loose ends are nailed securely to a rafter or to the plate. If ceiling joists run parallel to the house wall, special bracing must be installed. Brickwork is built around and over the ties.

15. ROOF PENETRATION

When the entire fireplace structure is built inside the house, the chimney penetrates the roof without touching the wooden framing in either the ceiling or the roof. So that the openings in the ceiling and roof will not weaken the house structure, rafters and ceiling joists are doubled around the open space. Woodwork is backed off 2 inches from the masonry. The open space should be closed over with metal to prevent a possible room fire from passing to the attic through the gap. The open area may be filled in with loose gravel, pumice, plaster chips, or other noncombustible materials. The space is never filled in solid with mortar. An interior chimney may be anchored to the rafters or ceiling joists, but this is not required.

16. ROOF FLASHING

At the point where the chimney passes through the roof, flashing is again needed to keep water from penetrating the house. First, wide strips of metal (copper, galvanized iron, aluminum) are cut and bent so one angle butts against the chimney, the other lies flat on the roof sheathing. Then, another layer of metal, known as cap or counter flashing, is cut and shaped to fit into the brickwork and overlap the first layer and thus conduct water over its exposed edges. Mortar joints are left partly open to receive the cap flashing, which is sealed in place with a caulking compound. Open joints are made watertight by soldering. When flashing is in place, the finished roofing is installed over the layer nailed to sheathing.

17. CHIMNEY CAP

The chimney top is carried up above the roof line —2 feet above a peaked roof, 3 feet above a flat one. The flue tile is brought 4 inches above the top of the brickwork and a smooth bevel troweled in place. A stiff mixture of sand and cement is used instead of mortar. The sloping collar causes water to run off instead of penetrating the brickwork, and it also encourages wind currents to roll off the chimney cap instead of flowing down the flue. A tile chimney pot or cap may be added either to raise the height of the flue or to serve as a baffle against the wind. If a spark arrester is installed, it should be removable for cleaning and replacement, and should be fashioned of a corrosion-resistant mesh.

How to add on a fireplace

Fireplaces can be added-on. It is not a simple job, and it is not an operation that can be done in one or two week ends—in fact, the clutter may well be with you for a month or two. There is the usual digging, mixing, and bricklaying that goes with any fireplace building job. But on top of that, the wall and floor have to be opened and their internal framing rebuilt so they will not be weakened. Finished handwork is required to mend the broken plaster, restore the finish flooring, and fit flashing around the chimney.

If you are building now and have to defer your fireplace, have your architect make provisions for it in foundation, framing, and roof structure so you can add it on later without too much toil.

The drawings that follow show how it is possible to add a very simple fireplace onto a typical one-story frame house. *These drawings are intended to serve as an introduction to the principles involved in adding on a fireplace, and should not be followed literally.*

The first step is to draw up plans and material lists. Refer to your house blueprints to determine if the dimensions of your fireplace will fit into existing framing and to make sure that you will not be cutting into plumbing, wiring, or furnace ducts. When your plans are complete, check them over with your building inspector.

1. LAYING OUT THE JOB

When you have decided on the spot for building the fireplace, draw lines on the outside wall where you are going to cut. Be sure to avoid laying the line over a stud. You can tell where studs are by pounding on the wall with a hammer (the stud responds with a solid thud), or by measuring from a nearby door or window (studs are usually set 16 inches on center), or by boring an exploratory hole or two. Then lay out the boundaries of your foundation pit with string. Since the foundation will have to be at least six inches larger all around than the chimney, allow yourself plenty of digging room. It will also pay you to crawl under the house to see what you are going to encounter when you open the floor.

2. DIGGING THE FOUNDATION PIT

Dig out the foundation pit to meet your boundary lines. Expose the concrete house foundation and dig down below and *under* it. The proper depth will depend upon local conditions—frost, soil type, building ordinances. Clear off the concrete foundation thoroughly. Build forms to hold the wet concrete to the exact outside dimension of the slab. Place ½-inch reinforcing steel in grid form, 12 inches on centers, 5 inches from the bottom of the pit. For added strength, set four steel rods vertically so they will extend up into the *inside* corners of the rough brick firebox. Allow concrete a day or so to cure. Keep covered with straw, dirt, sacking, and keep damp for a week or ten days.

3. OPENING THE WALL

Next step is to open the wall and expose the studs. First, bore a hole in each of the upper corners of the opening. Start cutting with a keyhole saw and transfer the job to a sturdy cross-cut that won't be ruined if it encounters some nails. Cut down to floor level and pry off the outside wall covering—siding, shingles, stucco board — remove the protective waterproof paper beneath it, then take out the diagonal sheathing. Cut open the inside wall and remove the laths or plasterboard. *Do not cut the studs*—just clear out everything around them, including any crossbracing. Better have a heavy tarpaulin near at hand to nail over the opening, for it will probably be gaping open for several days.

4. CUTTING THE STUDS

Don't forget that the studs are holding up your roof as well as keeping the wall in place. Before you cut them, therefore, make provision for carrying the load while the wall is open and temporarily weakened. One way is to transfer the load to a pair of 2x6's placed between floor and ceiling inside the room. To spread the load, butt ends of the uprights against 2x8 planks, one on the floor, one against the ceiling. Cut uprights about ¼ inch longer than the space measures and force them into position. When placing the ceiling cross-member, be sure it runs crosswise to ceiling joists; or if joists run in same direction as the fireplace wall, place cross-member so it rests under a joist—rather than between two of them.

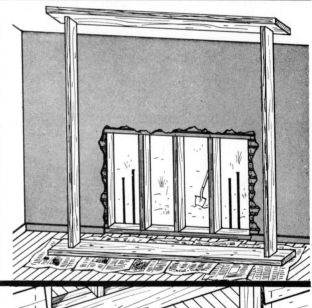

5. OPENING THE FLOOR

Before cutting into the floor, finish off the wall opening. Note how the finished opening is framed: the load formerly carried by the cut studs is dispersed along a pair of 2x6's, placed side by side over the top of the hole, and carried down to the sill along doubled studs on both sides. Doubled studding is also run up to the plate. Remember that once the floor joists are cut, the floor is weakened unless additional support is installed. Set a girder (6x6) under the joists *before they are cut.* Support it on posts resting on precast concrete piers. Leave girder and piers in place after floor is finished. If you wish to avoid cutting the floor, plan for a cantilevered, elevated hearth —but see your architect and building inspector first.

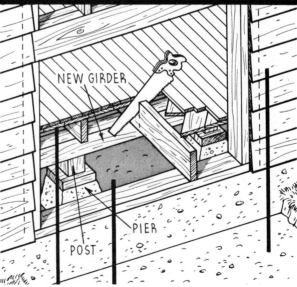

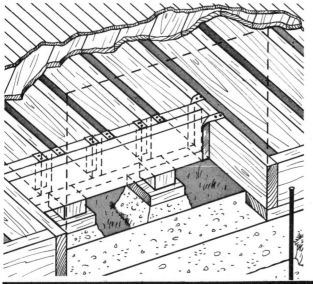

6. FINISHING THE FLOOR OPENING

Finish off floor construction by rebuilding floor sub-structure so it can carry the load once borne by the joists you have cut. First, measure and cut two lengths of timber to fit across the exposed ends of the cut joists and butt snugly against the uncut joists on both sides of opening. Nail firmly in place. As an optional step, support the ends of the cut joists in iron hangers, as shown in the drawing. If subflooring is easy to get at, you may want to double the joists on both sides of the opening. They should be doubled back to the first girder. This may not be a simple task, especially in an old house where wiring, plumbing, bridging and natural floor sag will interfere with running new joists that far back.

7. BUILDING THE ASH PIT

You are now ready to start the brickwork. Clean all dirt off the top of the concrete foundation slab so the mortar will stick to the slab. Lay a wall two bricks wide across the front and back, one wide on the sides. Butt the front wall against the foundation. The two short walls, inside the box, do not have to be locked into the structure. They support the firebox brick-work. Use Type B mortar. The vertical reinforcing rods should be bedded in masonry to protect them from rusting out. Lay bricks across the corners and fill in with grout. Be sure to mortar the clean-out door securely in place so hot embers will not escape.

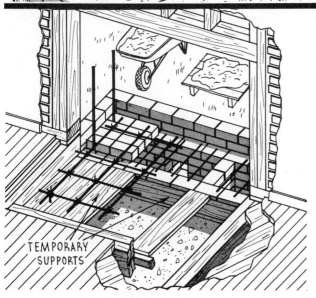

TEMPORARY SUPPORTS

8. FORMING THE SUBHEARTH

Ash pit finished, you are now ready to start the sub-hearth. Keep a wary eye on dimensions, to be sure that surface of the finished hearth comes out flush with the finish flooring. Figure down from the floor surface. Allow for the finished hearth (¾ inch for tile, 2¼ inches for brick), a bed of mortar (at least ½ inch), and at least 6 inches of concrete subhearth. Total: 7¼ to 8¾ inches. Wooden forms hold front hearth in place while concrete is setting; loose bricks, resting on ½-inch steel rods, support back hearth. Latter may also be supported on wood (remove through clean-out door after concrete sets), solid brickwork, or steel plates. Place a grid of reinforcing steel 3 inches below top of slab, and pour in concrete.

9. FINISHING THE FACING

When the hearth slab has set about 12 hours, you can start building on it. Build up the firebox (see details in the series of drawings in preceding chapter), place the damper in position, and build the facing. Don't forget to stop your masonry 2 inches below the wall cross-framing. To secure smooth mortar joints on the facing, use a mason's pointing trowel. Better practice with it on some rough brickwork first. Restore the inner wall surface with patching plaster or strips of wallboard. Lay the hearth up to the wood, then fill in the gap with strips of subflooring and cover with finish flooring, salvaged from that removed when you cut the floor.

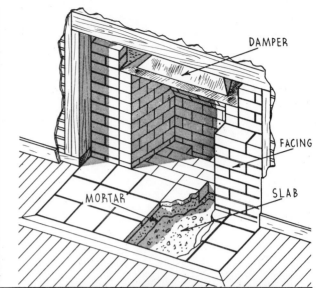

10. WEATHERSEAL

To make certain that water will not seep into the house around the edges of the fireplace opening, seal all points where masonry passes through woodwork. Around sides, where masonry butts against doubled studs, bricks should be laid against waterproof paper and then caulked with a mastic compound. Across the top of the firebox, metal flashing is needed to divert water away from the opening. Slip one angle of the flashing under outer wall covering, cover with weather-proof paper, and then nail on the finished covering. The angle of the flashing that fits into the brickwork should be mortared into a running joint and sealed with mastic. Top flashing is shaped to overlap sides to shed water at the corners.

11. BUILDING THROAT AND CHIMNEY

Brickwork on both sides of the firebox should be stepped in for six or seven courses until the throat narrows down to flue size. Lay last course to provide a slight ledge for flue tile to rest upon. Smooth off inner surface of stepped-in bricks to assist passage of flue gases. Fill in with mortar or bevel bricks. Before setting chimney, fasten weatherproof paper on house wall where bricks will rest against it. Cement the tiles in place and lay the bricks around them. (If bricks are laid first, the green masonry is likely to be damaged when the heavy tiles are positioned.) To cut a tile, place cement sack inside, fill tightly with sand, and sever with a series of cuts with a chisel.

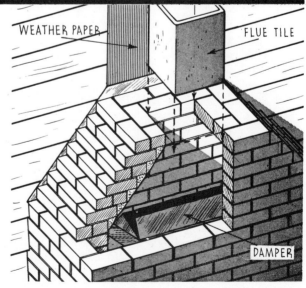

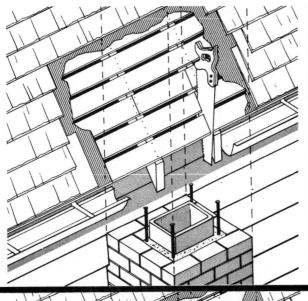

12. PENETRATING THE ROOF

At the point where the chimney passes the roof line, it is necessary to cut into the roof in order to install an anchoring device to brace the chimney. Clear away the shingle or composition roof surfacing for an area a good foot larger all around than the opening needed for the chimney. Mark cutting lines on roof sheathing 2 inches wider than each side of the masonry, and saw out the pieces. Remove enough of the sheathing so you can freely reach the plate. Cut off tips of rafters, if they extend beyond the roof line, flush with outside wall. If your house is equipped with gutters, cut them with a hacksaw. Note reinforcing steel in each corner of chimney masonry, sealed in with grout.

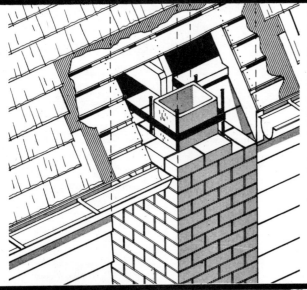

13. TYING-IN THE CHIMNEY

The chimney should be anchored to the house framing by some means. There are several ways to do this. In the drawing, a 1-inch iron strap is bent around a tile and the reinforcing steel, twisted to pass flat through a mortar joint, and nailed to the plate or a rafter. If ceiling joists run parallel to the wall, fasten cross members to the joists, as shown in the blueprint at the end of this book. Repair cut gutters by filing off rough edges and soldering caps on each of the cut ends. Be sure to buy caps of the same metal as the gutters, otherwise electrolytic reaction between the different metals will corrode edges and destroy the seal. (Also, better be sure that there is a downspout to drain each of the severed gutters.)

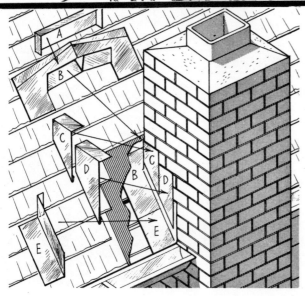

14. FITTING THE FLASHING

Install metal (copper, lead, galvanized iron, aluminum) flashing around chimney to seal the opening against water leakage. Flashing is applied in two layers. Bottom layer (B and E in drawing) is fitted under roof covering and bent to lay flat against the brickwork. Second layer (A, C, D in the drawing) is cemented and caulked into the masonry and fitted so it overlaps the first layer. This is known as cap flashing. Except where they overlap, flashing joints should all be soldered. Allow some leeway between cap and base flashing to permit chimney to settle or move slightly without rupturing the seal. Flashing along upside of chimney (B in drawing) should be bent up in the center—a finicky job for a sheetmetal shop.

WORKING DRAWINGS FOR CONSTRUCTION OF RESIDENTIAL FIREPLACE AND CHIMNEY

SUGGESTED MINIMUM CONSTRUCTION REQUIREMENTS

The following suggested requirements were developed as a guide to architects, building officials, masonry contractors, and others in establishing uniform minimum practices for the construction of residential fireplaces and chimneys.

A. GENERAL REQUIREMENTS

1. Fill all joints solidly with mortar or grout especially the joint between the flue lining and the surrounding masonry.

2. Mortar proportions, parts by volume.
     1 part cement
     ½ part lime putty or fire clay
    4½ parts clean sharp sand

3. Line all chimneys with a fire clay flue lining or 4" of fire brick.

4. Inside flue area and damper opening area shall each be at least 10% of fireplace opening area.

5. All reinforcing is to be thoroughly embedded in mortar or grout.

6. Throat should be drawn in at an angle between 45° and 60° with the horizontal.

7. Chimney should pass outside or inside of upper plate but should not cut through it unless adequate additional framing is provided. DETERMINE LOCAL REQUIREMENTS BEFORE PROCEEDING.

8. All masonry shall be bonded together by lapping one brick over another or by metal ties.

9. For chimneys enclosed by wood framing see Detail #4. Provide fire stop at ceiling line. Provide chimney tie at ceiling line or roof line as required by local Building Official.

10. Four ½-inch steel dowels are to be built into sub-hearth masonry.

(Continued on page 4)

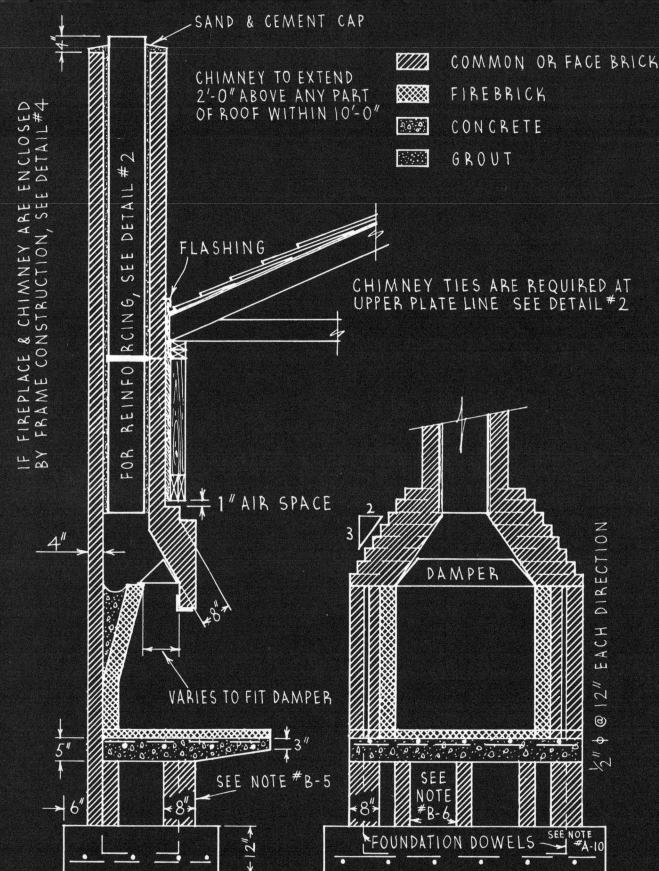

SAND & CEMENT CAP

CHIMNEY TO EXTEND
2'-0" ABOVE ANY PART
OF ROOF WITHIN 10'-0"

COMMON OR FACE BRICK
FIREBRICK
CONCRETE
GROUT

IF FIREPLACE & CHIMNEY ARE ENCLOSED
BY FRAME CONSTRUCTION, SEE DETAIL #4

FOR REINFORCING, SEE DETAIL #2

FLASHING

CHIMNEY TIES ARE REQUIRED AT
UPPER PLATE LINE SEE DETAIL #2

1" AIR SPACE

4"

2
3

DAMPER

1/2" φ @ 12" EACH DIRECTION

8"

VARIES TO FIT DAMPER

5"

3"

SEE NOTE #B-5

SEE
NOTE
#B-6

6"

8"

8"

12"

FOUNDATION DOWELS

SEE NOTE
#A-10

DETAIL #1 — SECTIONS THRU FIREPLACE AND CHIMNEY

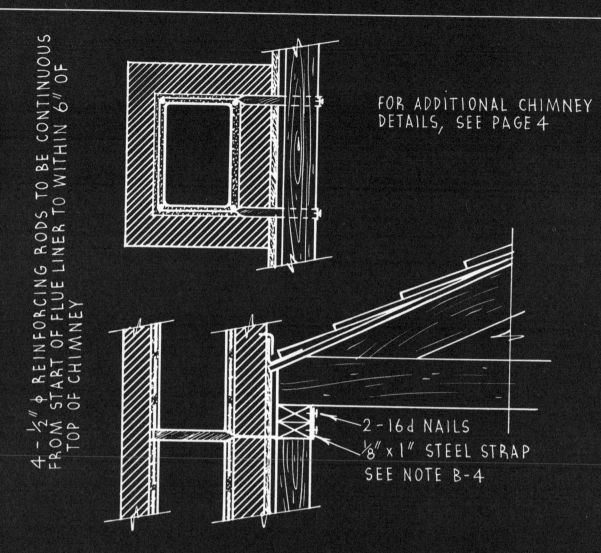

FOR ADDITIONAL CHIMNEY
DETAILS, SEE PAGE 4

4 – ½" φ REINFORCING RODS TO BE CONTINUOUS
FROM START OF FLUE LINER TO WITHIN 6" OF
TOP OF CHIMNEY

2 – 16d NAILS
⅛" × 1" STEEL STRAP
SEE NOTE B-4

DETAIL #2 — CHIMNEY SECTION & PLATE TIE DETAILS

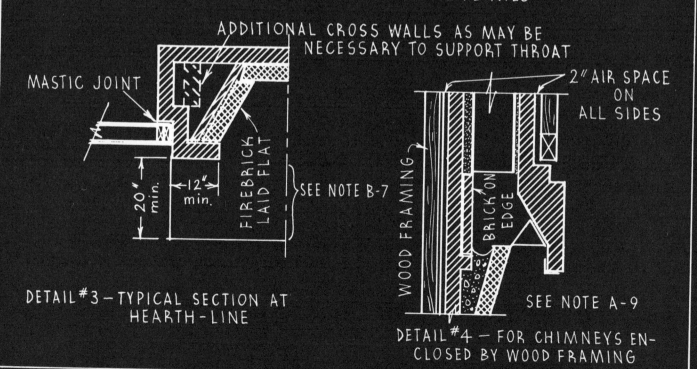

ADDITIONAL CROSS WALLS AS MAY BE
NECESSARY TO SUPPORT THROAT

MASTIC JOINT

2" AIR SPACE
ON
ALL SIDES

20" min.

12" min.

FIREBRICK LAID FLAT

SEE NOTE B-7

WOOD FRAMING

BRICK ON EDGE

SEE NOTE A-9

DETAIL #3 – TYPICAL SECTION AT
HEARTH-LINE

DETAIL #4 — FOR CHIMNEYS EN-
CLOSED BY WOOD FRAMING

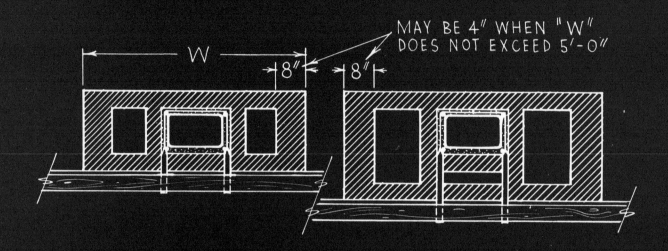

4

DETAIL #5 — FOR CHIMNEYS OF UNUSUAL WIDTH & THICKNESS

B. SPECIAL REQUIREMENTS

1. Chimneys in areas subject to earthquakes or high winds shall be adequately reinforced as required by the local Building Official.

2. Plans for types of fireplaces or details of construction not shown in these drawings should be submitted to the local Building Official for approval in advance of construction.

3. If the ceiling joists do not frame into the upper plate to which the fireplace is tied, additional bracing may be required. DETERMINE LOCAL REQUIREMENTS BEFORE PROCEEDING.

4. Some Building Departments require a different type of chimney tie than that shown. DETERMINE LOCAL REQUIREMENTS BEFORE PROCEEDING.

5. When the distance between the foundation and the hearth slab is less than 3'-0" supporting walls may be reduced to 4".

6. Some Building Departments require 4" supporting cross walls under the fire box and hearths if the latter is of unusual proportions. DETERMINE LOCAL REQUIREMENTS BEFORE PROCEEDING.

7. Where house has a concrete slab floor, hearth is to be raised or of dissimilar material.

The construction drawings on these pages were prepared by the Clay Brick and Tile Association, San Francisco, in cooperation with building officials of several municipalities.